How to stencil and decorate furniture and tinware

STENCILED AND PAINTED SHERATON
FANCY CHAIR FROM "CLEOPATRA'S BARGE"

How to
stencil and decorate
furniture and tinware

NANCY RICHARDSON

The Ronald Press Company • *New York*

Library of Congress catalog card number 56–13455

PRINTED IN THE UNITED STATES OF AMERICA

To Rich, with gratitude

Preface

I hope that this book will inspire you to begin painting and stenciling. Most of us are hesitant to begin a new craft which looks difficult without the aid of a teacher, yet the failures that beset beginners in this one may easily be avoided by using the right methods and materials.

Except for raw materials, a good design is the most essential item for a lovely stenciled or painted object. This book contains many designs complete with detailed instructions. If you follow the directions carefully you will have no difficulty in producing a finished piece, even though you may never have used a paintbrush or stencil before.

Specific information is given on each kind of decorating, whether it be fine brush-stroke painting, bold primitive painting, stenciling, delicate bronzing in gold or silver, or applying gold leaf. Read the general instructions on the type of decorating you wish to do, pick out one of the easier patterns at first, and then go to work. Within a short time you will begin to take liberties with the patterns, and before you know it will be designing variations of your own.

Collecting designs has been one of my constant pleasures since I first began the study of Early American decorating. Most of the designs in this book have been collected over the past decade. Friends have been very generous in allowing me to copy designs from old pieces of tin and woodenware. A number of patterns have been found on old family pieces from Vermont farms; others on objects acquired in out-of-the-way places. Museums are excellent sources for designs of all sorts.

There is a section of design motifs which can be used in combination to create your own designs (and which you may even carry over into other crafts such as textile painting or block printing). These have come from the widest variety of sources— from early French and Spanish embroideries, from old Chinese porcelains, from Indonesian costumes, from carvings in wood and stone, from printed European textiles, from French inlaid or painted furniture, from mosaics, and, of course, from nature.

Once you begin to paint or stencil, you will be design-conscious, and you will find designs on all kinds of decorative objects, on wallpaper, china, and textiles, on everything, wherever you go. Record designs on paper, if possible at the moment you see them, for it will help you both to feel good design and to keep the motif from slipping away from you.

To enjoy designs, think of the symbolism expressed by those who have created them. For example, in Pennsylvania German ("Dutch") art, two large leaves at the base of a floral design stand for the idea of God creating and upholding life and growth. Similarly, a group of three leaves together is a reminder of the Christian Trinity. The wavy lines which are the beauty of so many Pennsylvania German designs tell of the Spirit of God moving in the world, while the lily (often also the tulip) is the symbol for purity. As you use designs from different parts of the world and from different periods, seek to know their meanings, for such a study will enrich your art.

I wish to acknowledge my gratitude to the Society for the Preservation of New England Antiquities, Boston; the Essex Institute, Salem, Massachusetts; to the Metropolitan Museum of Art, New York; and to their staffs, who have been unfailingly helpful in enabling me to gather so complete a portfolio of Early

American designs. I am also indebted to the Smithsonian Institution, Washington, for the cooperation of its staff in providing me with materials from their collections from many lands, from which I sketched many design motifs that appear in the portfolio. I am also grateful to those who have arranged the collections of Oriental and European objects in the National Gallery of Art in Washington, from which I obtained many design ideas.

Above all, I acknowledge my deepest debt to those who have taught me the arts described in this book and who have been generous in sharing designs with me over a number of years. Since I began painting and stenciling under their kind and patient tutelage, I have wanted to share with others the pleasure that I found at once in decorating, and to provide patterns of all kinds for their use. I hope this book will help you discover your own latent talents, for I am convinced that anyone who can hold a paintbrush, and who will practice simple brush strokes patiently at first, can become a successful decorator.

NANCY RICHARDSON

Alexandria, Virginia
August, 1956

Contents

How to use this book

The chapters of this book are arranged, so far as possible, in the order in which you will be working.

First there is a chapter on getting started, in which you will find suggestions about things to decorate, and about choosing a suitable form of decoration for them. Then materials for different types of decoration are discussed (each type using many of the same materials as the other, of course). The types of decoration are described in the order in which they would be taught in a class. (Stenciling is near the end, but could actually be learned first, if desired.)

You will be decorating both new and old articles, so you will find in Chapter 2 instructions on how to get such articles ready for painting, staining, or varnishing, whether they are wood or metal.

Following this, you can read about painting metal (beginning with a metal priming coat) and painting or staining wood. In this chapter you can discover also how to produce some unusual background effects which were characteristic of early American decorating.

In Chapter 3, beginning with a design to be copied, you will learn how to change or enlarge the design and how to get it from a traced copy onto the material you are decorating.

In Chapter 4 you will learn how to use your brush. Pay close attention to all the *brush strokes* as well as how to paint curving lines and how to stripe; nearly every design requires the use of brush strokes and curving lines, with at least one stripe for trim.

Chapter 5 deals with colors. You will begin with a few simple colors, but you will want to know how to mix them. Later you will keep adding interesting colors to your paintbox, for special uses, so color is discussed here: colors are identified; you are told how to mix many colors useful in decorating wood and tinware; discussion of peasant colors and striping colors, and illustrations of a number of simple border and peasant designs, follow.

Chapter 6 takes up the use of gold, silver, and other metallic powders, except in the field of stenciling. You will learn how to apply your knowledge of brush strokes and line work, using the powders instead of oil colors with your varnish medium.

Designs suitable for painting in gold and silver, and for freehand bronze, are included. Freehand bronzing is the application of metallic powders to painted motifs, which has a resemblance to stenciling in its finished effect. Some of the same designs may be used for gold leaf, just as some of the smaller peasant designs in the previous section might be painted in gold.

Chapter 7 teaches you how to apply gold leaf, and how to etch or color it.

Chapter 8 is entirely on stenciling. It tells you how to trace a pattern on linen and to cut it out and apply it. It takes up the different types of stencil, transparent painting over stencils, and care of stencils.

The stencil designs begin with simple one-piece stencils, are followed by composite stencils, and end with a stenciled-and-painted design.

Chapter 9 gives some general information about painting natural flowers and fruit. (There is some specific information about painting the roses on the large Chippendale tray, illustrated in the chapter.

There are not many floral designs in this chapter because the sources, such as flower prints, magazine illustrations, etc., are numerous. One stylized pattern, the type of rose used on lace-edge trays, is included.

Chapter 10 shows you how to give the decorative work lasting perfection after you have chosen to do it by one of the foregoing methods. It describes how to achieve a satin-smooth but not shiny finish by means of varnish, carefully applied and afterwards rubbed down. In case you wish to make your work look old, or to subdue colors which are a bit too bright, there is advice here on coats of antiquing, which precede the final coat of varnish.

Chapter 11 tells how to paint a glass top for a mirror by an old process known as *reverse painting*. A primitive design taken from an antique mirror is included, but you may use your imagination in creating the scene to be painted. The variety is wide, and includes designs in gold leaf. The designs from Dutch tiles are unrelated, but are examples of the type of painting that might be applied to mirror tops. They could also be applied to small boxes or trays.

Last of all, but not least important, is a portfolio of design material, from which you can combine and create your own designs.

Although tracing and copying are mentioned often throughout the book, you will sooner or later wish to make some of your own patterns. You will acquire a feel for shape and design through painting and tracing that will make it easier than you may suspect to draw your own.

Use these patterns in many ways—they may be painted, stenciled, carved, embroidered, for they have come from a variety of pieces decorated by various methods.

*How to stencil and decorate
furniture and tinware*

CHAPTER

1

Getting started

At first, assemble only a few things with which to work, so that you will know their uses well.

I. *Things you will enjoy decorating*

You may begin by painting something very simple, such as a small tray from the variety store. On it you can learn how to create a good finish, and to do a simple brush stroke or stencil, with more ease than on a larger object.

There are, of course, all manner of things to decorate, most of them very close at hand. There are kitchen canisters, cookie cans, salad bowls, cookie sheets to be used as trays, and recipe boxes. A frozen orange juice can makes a glorified pencil holder for your desk or telephone table, while a typewriter ribbon box is a charming container, when decorated, for small things like paper clips or bobby pins.

If you hunt in attics and junk shops, you will come across such things as wooden chests and wooden buckets to decorate for use as kindling containers by the fireplace. Milk cans and other large containers become excellent lampbases. Old washstands and commodes make excellent telephone tables and wine cabinets, respectively.

II. *Choosing a suitable design*

Obviously, there is no end to the variety of things which may be charmingly improved by a painted or stenciled decoration. The only caution that must be given is not to overdo things. Gay peasant designs are very cheering in the kitchen, and on trays, boxes, and chests which are used for accent. For the average room, however, it is well in general to decorate objects in more subdued colors and designs. Designs must also be suited to the size and type of article. A delicate antique chair calls for a delicate design, possibly in gold, while a sturdy kitchen chair is entirely suited to a bold one in bright colors.

Gold and silver decoration is usually used on furniture and tinware which is either refined in style or small in size.

There is no absolute rule, except that the decoration be well related to the subject and its use.

III. *Materials for painting*

For tracing designs and for painting sample copies of them, you will need a 9×12 pad of tracing paper. Either French chalk in stick form, or lithopone (a smooth chalky powder) rubbed in with absorbent cotton, is used on the back of the tracing paper for transferring the design to the object. (Even ordinary chalk may be substituted, but it is not as smooth.) A silver pencil, run over the chalk lines on the article being decorated, will make the lines more easy to see.

At first, for painting you will need only a few tubes of artist's oil colors. You may purchase at first: American vermilion, cadmium yellow medium, Prussian blue, yellow ochre, raw umber, burnt umber, and drop black, as well as a large tube of titanium or flake white. (Later, you will want to add alizarin crimson and yellow lake, both transparent colors.) Secure a palette knife for mixing.

Two inexpensive square-tipped brushes, either quill or tray painter, in sizes #1 and #3, will be enough for painting brush strokes. Later a #3 scroller, such as the 831 series art sign brush, and a long-hair striping brush may be included.

A 1½″ or 2″ brush will be used for painting backgrounds, with red sanding primer and Valspar flat black enamel. Use a 1″ varnish brush to apply all coats of Supervalspar varnish. This same varnish is used (with turpentine or alone) with oil colors in painting designs. You will also need turpentine for thinning paint and cleaning brushes, and #0000 wet and dry sandpaper, crude oil, and rottenstone for rubbing down paint and varnish.

From supplies already in the house, collect small paint cloths (preferably from old sheets or other lint-free cotton), slick-paper magazines to use as palettes, a piece of heavy felt or flannel for applying oil and rottenstone, a basket or tackle box to hold your materials, an orange juice can to hold small brushes head up, tin bottle caps to hold varnish and turpentine, medium-soft lead pencils, disposable spoons for dipping out paint and varnish, and newspapers.

To begin painting, get out materials such as those listed in Chapter 4 and practice your brush strokes on a slick magazine until you feel ready to copy an easy pattern in paint. Trace a pattern such as the one on page 27 onto tracing paper and fasten it to a piece of cardboard. Follow the directions in Chapter 4 for painting in a design.

Now prepare the small tray or whatever you have chosen to decorate. If permanent results are not important, you may ignore the advice about entirely removing the coat of new paint on the bought article. Do, however, rub it evenly all over with a piece of #0000 wet and dry sandpaper which has been wet and rubbed on a wet cake of soap. Small bubbles and bits of dust in the original paint will disappear, making a good surface for painting. Now follow the directions for painting and varnishing metal as background for decorating (pp. 16–17), which tell you in detail how to apply and finish each priming, color, and varnish coat smoothly.

Practice mixing your oil colors before starting to decorate, using the suggestions for mixing given in Chapter 5. Experiment until you can mix the soft gray-green of leaves and the other colors you will need. Now paint your design directly on the tray, just as you did on the tracing paper, using it as a guide.

A coat or several coats of varnish, according to the amount of wear a piece will get, always goes over the decoration to protect it. Chapter 10 will give you instructions for giving your tray a smooth but dull finish.

IV. *Materials for painting in gold and similar materials*

For painting in gold, silver, copper, and other so-called bronze powders, you will need the same assortment as that described in the previous section, except for oil colors. Of these you will need only a few, for small painted touches on or around the gold design.

Two shades of gold: a pale gold—such as Venus #57 Pale Gold Lining—and another, deeper gold—such as brushed brass or rich gold—are enough for most designs in gold. The "lining" bronzes are always very fine powders. *Never* buy coarse powders such as those sold in variety stores. All the bronzes, including chromium, aluminum, brilliant fire, copper, and the like are taken up at the beginning of Chapter 6.

You will also want some flat jar lids on which to put the powders and a soft water-color brush with which to brush on dry gold after your painted work is nearly dry.

First paint the article with a priming coat, color coats, and varnish coat according to the directions for painting and varnishing as a background for decorating (pp. 16–19). Then apply your design in gold or silver, following the instructions for painting with bronze powders. Follow with the varnish coats, as directed in Chapter 10 (pp. 157–160).

V. *Materials for freehand bronzing*

These are the same as for painting in gold, with the addition of a small can of black Serviceseal varnish, if obtainable, and a small hemmed piece of firm silk velvet (heavy silk millinery velvet is best), a soft thick piece of chamois, or a soft, round-tipped water-color brush of best quality, for applying the powder.

The article is first given its prime, color, and varnish coats. Then follow the directions in Chapter 6 for freehand bronzing on painted motifs. Finish with the varnish coats; directions are given in Chapter 10 (pp. 157–160).

VI. *Materials for applying gold leaf*

Gold leaf is applied over a design which has been painted in gold, so you will need the same #1 and #3 square-tipped tray painter or quill brushes, a scroll brush if there are fine lines in the design, very fine pale gold lining bronze, and Supervalspar and turpentine. Besides these you will need a packet of gold or aluminum leaf, and waxed paper, if the leaf is not applied to thin waxed paper when you buy it. A bit of absorbent cotton or velvet is useful.

If you plan to etch the details into the gold leaf, you will find helpful a little tool called a pin vise, which will hold a phonograph needle or any sharp point. Or you may make your own by imbedding a phonograph needle in a short stick. You can also paint in the details with a #1 or #0 pointed quill brush, or draw them in with a crow-quill (croquille) pen and waterproof, varnishproof India ink. For shading the gold leaf motifs, burnt umber artist's oil color is used with varnish and turpentine, applied with a #2 or #3 brush.

For transparent washes of color over gold leaf, use the three transparent oil colors: Prussian blue, alizarin crimson, and yellow lake, plus burnt umber and a touch of raw umber.

Chapter 7 gives complete instructions for gold leaf work. First give the article its prime, color, and varnish coats. Then follow directions for gold leaf and for applying details, shading, transparent color washes, and so forth in Chapter 7. Follow with the varnish coats, following the directions given in Chapter 10.

VII. *Materials for stenciling*

In order to cut out your own stencils you will need architect's linen and a very sharp, pointed pair of embroidery or manicure scissors. Cutting a bit of very fine sandpaper will help sharpen them. Trace the pattern onto the semitransparent bluish linen with pen and India ink, in order to have a good clear line to cut.

For the actual stenciling, you will need good varnish and a soft varnish brush. Stencil with a firm piece of silk velvet, such as heavy millinery velvet, so that the fine bronze powder cannot sift through it (hem it before using). A soft piece of chamois might also be used. Two or three bronze powders will be enough at first: pale gold lining bronze such as Venus #57, rich gold, or brushed brass and chromium. They must be so fine that they will adhere to the sides of a glass bottle (lining bronzes are always very fine). If you can find a heavy piece of drapery velour, you can line up several colors of bronze along the inside fold and store it with your supplies that way. Turpentine and Carbona plus some lintless cloths complete the list. (There is a longer list of bronze powders in Chapter 8.)

You will need, as well, a good quality 1½″ paint brush, red sanding primer, and Valspar flat black enamel for the priming and color coats. The same varnish and varnishing brush are used for all varnishing. Prepare the basic coats, following directions for painting and varnishing as a background for decorating in Chapter 2. (One varnish coat is applied *before* the stenciling varnish.) Follow stenciling directions, Chapter 8. Finish the tray with varnish coats applied and rubbed according to directions in Chapter 10.

VIII. *Where to purchase supplies*

Most of the materials for preparing the surfaces to be painted, and for painting and finishing them, are found in hardware stores. Bronze powders, decorating brushes, and artist's oil colors should be purchased from an art supply dealer because it is important to get the best grade of each, often unknown to hardware dealers. Tracing paper, crow-quill pens, and India ink, as well as silver pencils, can usually be found at either a stationery store or an art supply store. Architect's tracing linen may be a little harder to find, but stationers carry it in some localities, and so do art dealers. Fine dental pumice and crude oil (used for the final rubbing of the varnish) can both be bought at drugstores.

2

Cleaning articles before painting; applying finish

I. Cleaning metal articles

Whether old or new, most metal articles should be cleaned of paint down to the bare surface. An old coat of paint is likely to be dried out and will chip easily, or rust may be eating the metal beneath the paint. In the case of new paint, it may have been applied over shellac, which will cause it to chip easily.

1. *Of paint, varnish, or varnish stain*

To remove these finishes, use one of the following methods.

A. Lye method

Materials: Lycons lye
Tongs
Steel wool
Vinegar

Use an enamel vessel for the lye; it is corrosive to metal. If possible, do the work outdoors. Shake a can or two of lye into very hot water.

Warning: be extremely careful of your eyes and skin while using lye.

Using long-handled tongs, immerse the metal articles in this bath. New paint softens quickly; old paint may take several hours to become loose. When the paint softens, scrub it off with steel wool held with long tongs. When the paint has all been removed, take the article from the bath. Wash it with half vinegar and half water, then with soap and water. Dry it immediately. Repaint as soon as possible, as rust forms quickly on bare metal.

B. Paint remover method

> *Materials:* Paint remover
> Old brush
> Steel wool #000
> Neutralizer for after-use specified on container
> Rubber gloves

Brush on the remover—one coat if the paint is fairly new, several at fifteen-minute intervals if the paint is stubborn to remove. When the paint begins to bubble up, scrape it off with steel wool, or with a scraper or palette knife. Clean the article according to the directions printed on the can, so that the remover will not keep on working through a new coat of paint. The neutralizer is usually benzene or naphtha. Do not apply new paint until the article has been thoroughly aired.

Warning: most removers are quite toxic and should be used only where there is plenty of fresh air.

C. Sal soda method

This does not work on a stubborn coat of paint, but is a very easy way to remove paint from cheap articles. Dissolve a good quantity of sal soda in very hot water and immerse the article until the paint softens. Remove the paint with steel wool. Wash with strong soap and water.

D. Trisodium phosphate method

This has the same limitations as sal soda. Dissolve plenty of trisodium phosphate in water near the boiling point. Immerse the article in this near-boiling solution until paint softens. Wash off with strong soap and water.

2. *Of rust*

After cleaning off the paint, rust may be found on the metal. Steel wool will remove light rust spots. Emery cloth may be carefully used to remove deeper rust. It is best to use a preparation called Rusticide for difficult-to-remove rust, *after* using the above methods. Rusticide also helps to inhibit rust from forming. Any rust left on will eventually eat through your decoration.

3. *Of residue on new metals*

Most new metals have a residue on them from manufacturing processes which may be unfavorable to paint. Use the following special treatments.

A. Aluminum

Remove aluminum stearate usually present by immersing article in a near-boiling solution of 1¼ pound trisodium phosphate to 1 quart water. Allow the article to dry and wash with clear water. The surface will be slightly etched by this treatment and will hold paint well.

B. Tin

Etch the surface lightly by sanding with fine sandpaper or steel wool.

C. Galvanized iron

Wash the iron with acetic acid, then in clear water. This removes the greasy zinc stearate.

II. *Cleaning paint and varnish from wooden articles*

Unless painted or varnished wood is in excellent condition, strip the piece entirely by one of the following methods, and begin with a new undercoat.

1. *Paint remover method*

Materials: Paint remover and an old brush
Steel wool #000
Neutralizer specified on can
Rubber gloves

Brush the remover thickly over a small portion of the piece and leave on according to directions printed on the can. If paint does not show signs of lifting or bubbling after fifteen minutes, apply two or three successive coats, allowing fifteen minutes between. Do not let it dry out, as this seems to drive the old finish into the wood grain. When the finish is well softened, take it off carefully with steel wool or some type of scraper. Sharpen a scraper on a stone every few minutes, but avoid gouging the wood. Use a two-sided file, or a piece of glass, on difficult turnings. Use steel wool on convex surfaces. The finish must be *completely* removed. Clean the surface with the neutralizer suggested on the can, usually turpentine, naphtha, or benzene, to prevent the remover acting on the new finish you apply. If the surface is not entirely smooth, go over it with fine steel wool.

2. *Dry-scraping method*

> *Materials:* Kitchen knife, jackknife, or wood scraper
> Sharpening stone
> Cotton gloves

This method is best on old, crackling paint or varnish. Care must be taken not to mar the wood. Scrape with the grain when possible. Use a two-sided file for difficult turnings. To protect your hands from being cut, wear heavy cotton gloves. Avoid inhaling the dust of the old finish.

3. *Lye method*

> *Materials:* Lycons lye
> Long-handled brush
> Rubber gloves
> Vinegar
> Sandpaper

Dissolve half a can of lye in an enamel pail of hot water. Place the furniture, or whatever you are stripping, over a drain in the garage, over an unused sandpile, or somewhere the lye can do no damage. Wear rubber gloves and old clothes, and be extremely careful of your eyes and of lye on your skin: it burns.

Using a long-handled brush, work the solution all over the piece, paying special attention to cracks and crevices. Go over it all at once to start it softening, then scrub with the brush, dipping it in the solution often. You will be able to see when the color or varnish is all gone. Rinse once with clear water, using a hose if possible for large pieces. Then pour over it a solution of half vinegar and half water, which restores the appearance and color of the wood grain. Be sure to cover every spot. Allow the article to dry for a few days until you are sure that even the crevices have dried out. Sandpaper any rough spots.

Do not apply lye to furniture more than *once*.

4. *Trisodium phosphate method*

> *Materials:* Trisodium phosphate
> Long-handled brush

Apply a strong solution of trisodium phosphate to any paint you feel sure will come off easily—it is not a strong paint remover. The chemical must be dissolved at near-boiling point, and cooled slightly. Do not leave it on long enough to swell the wood. Wash well with water and dry quickly. Sandpaper any rough spots.

III. *Painting and varnishing metal as a background for decorating*

Choose good soft brushes, and clean them perfectly after each use. To clean: press out paint between folds of clean newspaper. Then immerse in paint thinner well up to the seat of the bristles. Preferably, have several jars of thinner; the thinner can be poured off the sediment later and reused. Remove all the paint you can in the first jar, then place brush in a second one, and so on until no paint can be seen in the bristles. I also wash mine under running warm water, first wiping in one direction only on a cake of wet Ivory soap, then working the soap with my fingers into the bristles.

1. *The priming coat*

> *Materials:* Red sanding primer, an iron oxide primer used also
> as a primer on automobiles
> Zinc chromate metal primer, under pale colors
> (light gray)
> 1½″ or 2″ paint brush
> Turpentine
> Wet and dry #0000 sandpaper, or piece of heavy
> felt or flannel; crude oil and rottenstone

A good metal primer will cling tightly to the surface, will inhibit rust in iron or tin, and will make a surface which will hold subsequent coats of paint without flaking or chipping. Metal primer is usually thick as it comes in the can. Thin to the consistency of heavy cream. If the top layer on the can thickens, it may be lifted off with a palette knife.

Warm the paint by setting it in a coffee can of hot water. Paint in long, even strokes. In painting a tray, paint first the underside of the rim, then inside the rim. Pick up drops of paint that run down to the floor of the tray, then paint the floor with long, smooth strokes, brushed lengthwise. On an oval tray, swish the tip of the brush around the edge of the floor of the tray, if necessary. As you paint, blow on your work. This helps to settle and smooth it.

Let the primer dry for 24 hours in a warm and dust-free place, or longer if required. When dry, rub the article with #0000 wet and dry sandpaper, getting it wet and soapy before using. Rub very gently and evenly only to remove any imperfections in the surface, and to smooth the graininess of the primer. If the surface is already quite smooth, you may instead rub with a heavy piece of felt, dipped in crude oil and in rottenstone or dental pumice.

2. *Color coats*

> *Materials:* Flat enamel, or
> Japan paint (less durable), thinned to the consistency of thin cream with turpentine
> 1½″ or 2″ good paint brush
> Piece of heavy felt, rottenstone, and crude oil

Warm the paint. Apply evenly in long strokes, as above. Allow to dry 24 to 48 hours. Rub evenly and gently with a heavy piece of felt that has been dipped into crude oil, and lightly in rottenstone or in dental pumice until any bubbles or raised places are gone.

Apply two (or preferably three) thin coats, rubbing between coats as described.

3. *Varnishing over flat coats*

> *Materials*: Soft varnish brush, 1″–1½″ wide, reserved for this use only
>
> Good spar varnish, such as Supervalspar or—if available—use Clear Serviceseal varnish for this coat
>
> Piece of heavy felt or heavy flannel
>
> Dental pumice or rottenstone
>
> Crude oil or wet and dry sandpaper #0000

A coat of good varnish is always applied over the background color, not only to protect it, but to give a smooth base on which to paint your decoration; errors made in the course of decorating may be wiped off without damaging the base coats of paint, also.

Varnishing should be done in a room where the temperature is at least 70° so that the volatile oils in the varnish will evaporate before the varnish sets. Damp weather will slow drying, so avoid doing work then. A room without rugs or other materials to which dust can cling is the best environment for varnishing.

A varnishing brush is usually camel's hair or sable, and is much softer and more flexible than an ordinary paint brush. The varnish should not be used if it is old, or at all gummy. Never leave the can open.

Warm the varnish by setting the can in a coffee can of hot water. Take out a few spoonfuls into a clean jar cap. Apply it with long, smooth strokes. Blow on your work to smooth it as you apply the varnish. If bubbles occur, stroke them out in the same lengthwise direction. Once the varnish begins to set, do not touch up any spots.

To avoid bubbles: Do not shake or stir the can

Do not dip your brush in the can and wipe it on the edge

Press out bubbles found in your brush by pressing between folds of newspaper

Dry the varnished article in a warm, dust-free room for 24 to 48 hours, or until no trace of "tackiness" remains.

Rub evenly and gently with a heavy piece of felt dipped in crude oil, then lightly in rottenstone. This will remove the high gloss and leave the varnish very smooth. Wash with warm water and Ivory soap.

If there are any bubbles in the dry varnish, use wet and dry sandpaper instead of pumice or rottenstone. Wet the paper, apply it to a cake of wet soap, and rub very gently all over, either in long, smooth strokes, or with an all-over small circular motion.

IV. *Painting and staining woods as background for decorating*

1. *Painting wood*

Materials: Same as for painting metal, substituting undercoat for primer.

After filling all holes and cracks with plastic wood or putty, sand the surface and wipe clean with turpentine or paint thinner.

Use enamel undercoat as a first coat on wood. It fills the wood pores with a special penetrating oil, carrying the pigment in with it. It also contains a surfacing oil which prevents pitch and the like from seeping out of the wood, if the wood is new. Apply it quite thickly—as it comes in the can.

Do not shellac. Paint experts say that shellac raises the grain, making sanding difficult. Shellac also lacks oil, therefore chips easily and does not provide a good gripping surface for enamel.

When the undercoat is dry, sand it thoroughly. Follow it with two or more coats of semigloss enamel, sanding between coats. Rub down the final coat with damp cotton dipped in dental pumice, or with #0000 steel wool or trimite paper, or with finest wet and dry sandpaper, used wet with soap, using a steady circular motion, being careful not to rub too hard. (The undercoat may be followed with two coats of flat paint and one coat of varnish, if desired.)

2. *Staining wood*

Painted designs of peasant type are very attractive applied over natural wood finishes, which are achieved either by the alcohol-stain method (subsequently varnished) or the varnish-stain method.

A. Alcohol-stain method

> *Materials:* Alcohol stain
> Spar varnish
> Varnish brush
> #0000 steel wool, or pumice and absorbent cotton

Alcohol stain comes in a variety of wood tones—light and dark maple, colonial (soft red) mahogany, dark mahogany, and so forth. Wipe the stain on quickly with a soft cloth and wipe off immediately with a clean soft cloth. If a darker shade is desired, apply the stain again and again until a satisfactory color is obtained. The stain soaks in quickly and is difficult to remove, so apply lightly several times rather than all at once.

Allow the wood to dry thoroughly, varnish it, then rub down, following the directions given elsewhere in this chapter.

B. Varnish-stain method

> *Materials:* Varnish stain
> Varnish brush
> #0000 steel wool, or fine pumice and absorbent cotton

Varnish stain also comes in many wood colors, but it is a little more difficult to control the exact degree of color desired, as can be done by repeated applications of alcohol stain. This is especially true on wood furniture which may be made of more than one kind of wood, each requiring a different amount of color.

Apply varnish stain with a brush, like varnish. When completely dry, rub it down, using one of the methods described in this chapter.

V. *Common background colors on antique furniture*

Background colors for old country pieces were commonly dark red (now called *barn red*), dark blue, soft blue or blue-green, dark green or golden brown—the latter sometimes mottled in brown. Old chests frequently had ivory panels, elaborately decorated, applied against these colors. Frances Lichten, in her book on Pennsylvania German chests, suggests buying house paint in these colors and graying it with raw umber, after adding white or black as desired for light or darker tones. Thin this paint with linseed oil.

New England country furniture was commonly painted a mellow mustardy yellow, described as "country" or "old" yellow in Chapter 5.

Hitchcock chairs were usually grained to imitate mahogany. Formal types of stenciling were found on wood painted and veined to look like walnut. Fancy Sheraton chairs shared these trick effects or were painted in delicate colors, such as gray, pale green, ivory, or—rarely—red.

VI. *Common background colors on old tinware*

A few of the commonly used colors for tinware backgrounds are the following japan, or "coach-painter's" colors. They are often used with the addition of oil colors.

Permanent red : a warm, orange red
Tuscan red : brick red
Chrome yellow medium : yellow gold
Prussian blue : dull blue when grayed with raw umber
Chrome green medium : good dark green when mixed with black
Coach-painter's green : lovely deep blue-green
Ivory drop black : good warm black

The insides of old tin boxes were frequently painted with varnish to which a little transparent color had been added. For a bright sapphire blue, add a little good Prussian blue oil color to clear spar varnish and paint on very evenly. Streaks are very noticeable in transparent coats. Rather than have it too dark, use two light coats. Golden color is achieved by adding a little burnt sienna or burnt umber to clear varnish. Transparent ruby color is made by adding a little alizarin crimson or crimson lake oil color to varnish, with a drop of black as well.

For a copper luster effect, add a little black asphaltum (which is not black) and a touch of alizarin crimson oil color to varnish. The asphaltum may be purchased at hardware stores. It must be thinned with a little turpentine and applied with a sure stroke, as it does not flow like varnish and cannot be worked over after application. When thoroughly dry, rub down the coat of asphaltum by one of the methods described on page 159 and varnish. Rub very gently, as the asphaltum makes the varnish susceptible to scratching. Two coats may be used if desired, but it must be varnished over *before* any decoration is applied, as new coats of paint will soften it up.

VII. *Unusual backgrounds on old furniture and toleware*

1. *Mahogany or tortoise-shell background*

Paint the first coat or coats Venetian red, permanent red, or vermilion japan color, dulled with a little black or raw umber if necessary. Allow to dry, then brush on a thin coat of japan black or flat black. While wet, take a piece of clean, crumpled newspaper or other soft paper, or a piece of mosquito netting. Wipe the wet surface unevenly, creating the effect of natural wood grain where the red shows through. A soft brush is sometimes used to get the same effect. Allow to dry thoroughly and apply varnish. If the pattern looks too bright, a little burnt umber or asphaltum may be used to darken the varnish. On old chairs, the wide cross slat of the back was usually left plain black for stenciling.

2. *Imitation walnut-grained background*

This effect is not beautiful in itself, but was frequently used on pre-Victorian and Victorian furniture made of the cheaper woods. It might be interesting, or useful, to know how it was done.

The background is painted light brown in color and allowed to dry. A saw-tooth comb made of stiff cardboard or thin wood —as used in berry baskets—is dipped lightly in flat black paint. Draw it over the brown background in wavy lines to resemble walnut grain. You may cut a paint brush in points to do this also. When the black is thoroughly dry, coat it with varnish that has been darkened with burnt umber or asphaltum. It is better to put on several thin coats of darkened varnish than to give a muddy effect by adding a great deal of brown to the first coat applied.

3. *Mottling, usually over yellow paint*

Paint the background with yellow ochre japan color. When dry, roughly wipe on or brush on varnish to which has been added burnt sienna and raw umber tube color. A roll of putty, a soft cloth, or even a corncob—as suggested by Frances Lichten —may be used to produce patterns in the paint by pressing them into the sticky finish and allowing the background of dull yellow to show through. Patterns resembling fans, cirrus cloud effects, or any pattern may be made, as in modern finger painting, by pressing the putty, cob, or cloth where you wish the background to show through. Be sure to keep the putty or other tool with which you press clean. With putty, the dirty part may be kneaded inside of the roll until completely used. According to the skill you acquire, the results will be intriguing—or simply untidy.

Sometimes a mixture of vinegar and sugar, combined with a little powdered umber, is used in place of the colored varnish. It dries more slowly and is easier to manipulate.

Cover each of these finishes with a coat of varnish, and rub it down with pumice and water.

4. *Opaque crackled finishes*

Crackled paint, to give an effect of age, is made by using a very *short* (lacking in oily vehicle, such as flat paint) paint for the undercoat. Paint the top coat in enamel into which some naphthalene has been dissolved.

Tracing, altering, and transferring patterns

I. Tracing patterns

The first step in decorating is applying the outlines of your chosen design to tracing paper. Often the design must be reduced or enlarged to proper scale, or units of it must be left out or repeated in order to fit it to a given space. In any case cut a paper pattern of the space to be decorated out of tracing paper. Place it over your design to see what changes are necessary.

1. Reducing and enlarging patterns

If the pattern needs reducing slightly, draw *inside* each motif, on the tracing paper, rather than exactly on the lines of the design. (For greatly changing the size of a design, block it off in squares, then draw an equal number of squares on another piece of paper—larger squares for enlarging the design, smaller squares for reducing it. Number the squares on the original, as well as the new, blocks, and copy what is in each old block to the new spaces, and you will find your design complete in the required scale.) To increase the size of a design slightly, you will have to draw *outside* each motif, and slide the design over a little beneath the tracing paper to allow for the added size.

You may wish to change the arrangement of design somewhat, leaving the principal motifs unchanged, but repeating some of the smaller ones, and spacing large motifs farther apart. Decide first how the principal motifs shall be spaced, then fill in with more details, or use fewer of them, as necessary.

Trace with a sharp, hard pencil. Use the most transparent tracing paper you can buy; there is a great difference in transparency among papers. When your design has been copied onto tracing paper as you want it, you are ready to transfer it onto the object itself, by one of the following methods.

II. *Transferring designs*

1. *To dark backgrounds*

The design will, of course, have to be transferred in white or a light color in order to be seen against a dark background. All of the following materials are acceptable for use, though the powders are a little more trouble as the surplus powder must be wiped away. French chalk is probably the easiest to use.

A. French chalk outlines on back of tracing

Outline the design on the wrong side of the tracing paper with French chalk. Fasten the tracing to the article with masking

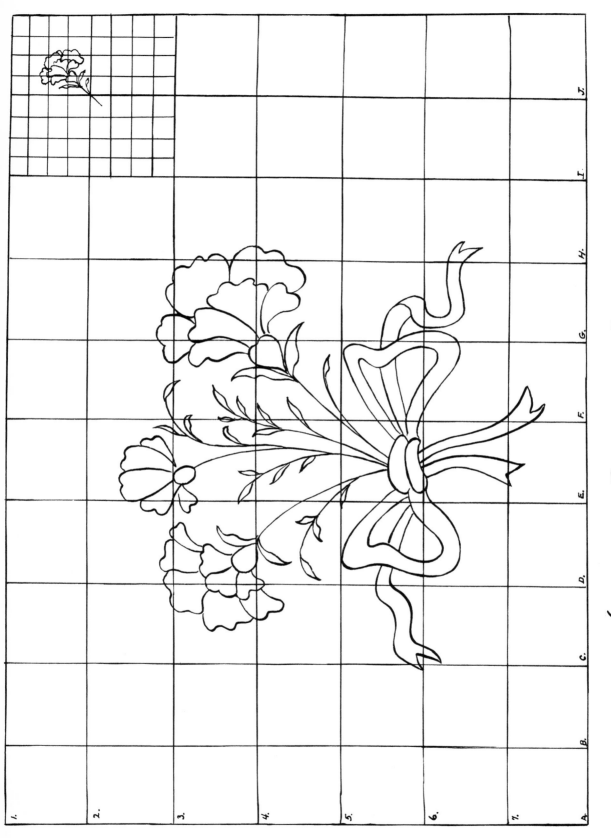

GRAPH FOR ENLARGING A DESIGN

tape, and press lightly with a stylus or sharp knitting needle or hard pencil over all the design except details which first coats would hide. Remove the tracing and go over the chalk lines with silver pencil.

B. Lithopone or powdered chalk rubbed over back of tracing

Rub the back of the tracing with a wad of absorbent cotton that has been pressed into lithopone, talcum, carbonate of magnesia, or chalk. Then fasten tracing to the article with masking tape. Press lightly with stylus, sharp knitting needle, or sharp, hard pencil over all the design except details which first coat covers. Remove tracing, and go over chalk lines with silver pencil.

C. Pounced lines (not greatly used)

Pierce the entire design on tracing paper with a coarse needle. Fasten design to article with masking tape. Pat through the pierced lines with a pounce (piece of cloth containing lithopone or talc). Go over the pounced lines, after removing tracing, with silver pencil.

D. Carbon paper tracing

Carbon paper comes in light, as well as dark, colors. Use orange-colored paper against all dark backgrounds. It may also be used against a gold background.

Insert the carbon paper beneath the tracing, shiny side down. Trace the design on the right side of the tracing paper with a stylus, hard pencil or a knitting needle.

The disadvantage of a carbon paper is its greasiness. If one rests one's hand on the carbon tracing while painting, it is likely to smear. It also smears when you are wiping off painting errors, and sometimes prevents the paint from adhering properly.

2. *To light backgrounds*

A. Graphite paper

Use graphite paper in the same way carbon paper is used. Graphite paper is less greasy, and quite satisfactory.

B. Soft pencil outlines on back of tracing

Use a heavy soft pencil and follow the lines of the design on the back of the tracing paper. Fasten the paper to the article with masking tape. Press lightly over the lines of the design with a stylus, sharp knitting needle, or sharp, hard pencil.

CHAPTER

Painting brush strokes and lines

Materials: #1 and #3 square-tipped quill or tray painter brushes
#0 or #1 pointed quill, or 831 art sign #0, or #1 scroller
Artist's oil colors listed for beginners, this chapter
Medium, made of half varnish and half turpentine
Varnish
Slick magazines for palette and for practice surface; newspapers to place under your work
Palette knife, turpentine, paint rags

Warm the medium first by setting bottle in a can of warm water.

Pour a little medium (which should be kept in a tightly shut bottle) into a small bottle cap. Pour turpentine into another. Have a lintless paint rag handy. Now put a dab of each needed oil color onto one edge of your magazine-palette. Use a large dab of white for mixing. (How to mix colors is discussed in the next chapter.) A thin, flexible palette knife is excellent for mixing.

31

FINE BRUSH STROKES AND LINEWORK

Dip #3 brush into medium, then touch it to the blended color and brush it back and forth a little in the color until it is flat and smooth. Do not get paint in the hilt of the bristles. Stroke surplus paint out on a newspaper, and begin to practice the following brush strokes. Most of the designs in the group which come next are made up of these brush strokes. Even elaborate gold border designs are made up of scrolls and curved motifs created by combinations of these same strokes.

I. *The rounded brush stroke*

Brush: #3 square-tipped quill or tray painter brush

Fill the brush and wipe it out on a magazine as above. Now, with the heel of your hand resting on the magazine, and using your little finger as a pivot, grasp the handle of the brush firmly.

Squash the tip of the brush on the magazine at a slight angle and allow the paint to settle there. When there is a slight puddle of paint, press to the left, with considerable pressure, then whip the brush toward you and up, on its edge, ending the curve toward the right on the nearest point of the square tip.

Practice doing this in the same direction for some time. When you have mastered the curved stroke in one direction, then start by pressing your brush toward the right after letting the paint settle, and bring it toward you and to the left, ending on the tip of the brush again.

If you will practice these rounded brush strokes for a good half hour each day, you will acquire a natural easy way of doing them which will bring grace to all your painting. There is hardly a painted design which does not make use of the rounded brush stroke, and you will find them combined in countless ways.

II. *The pointed brush stroke*

Brush: #3 square-tipped quill or tray painter brush

Again, with the heel of your hand on the magazine and your little finger as a pivot, grasp the brush tightly. Hold it at an angle to the paper and let a corner of the brush touch the paper first. Quickly draw it along a little, then press the brush down and to the left as you reach the center of the stroke, allowing the paint to flow onto the surface of the paper for a few seconds; then whip the brush in a reverse curve (*right,* then *left*) up onto its point. When this stroke becomes easy, make the same stroke in the opposite direction.

Practice a variety of leaf shapes with this stroke. The wave and chain designs, frequently seen on early American toleware, consist of a series of these strokes. There are many other variations. Try some of those shown when you have mastered the basic stroke. The chain design is frequently seen with the thick part of the stroke shaded in another color.

III. *Curving lines*

Brush: Scroller, such as 831 art sign #1 or #3, or #1 pointed quill brush

Take your fine-pointed brush and dip the tip into varnish. Wipe out on a cloth and dip it in oil color. Hold the brush nearly vertical. Steady your hand by resting its weight on your little finger tip. Draw the brush out along a piece of paper to see if the paint flows properly.

Now follow a curving line pattern with your brush, holding its tip at a right angle to the surface, and pressing slightly on it as you draw it along. When it runs out of paint, dip it in again and repeat the preparation of the brush. Now lay it about half an inch back of where you finished painting, in order to make a

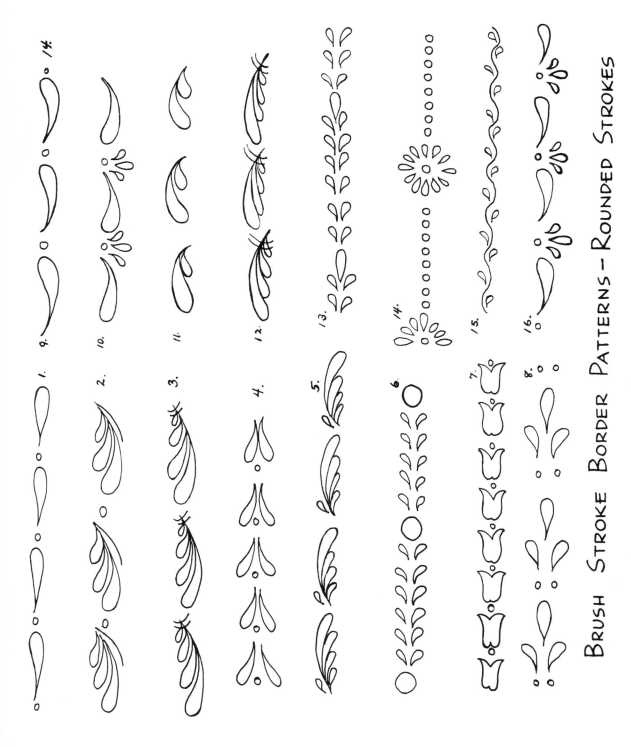

BRUSH STROKE BORDER PATTERNS — ROUNDED STROKES

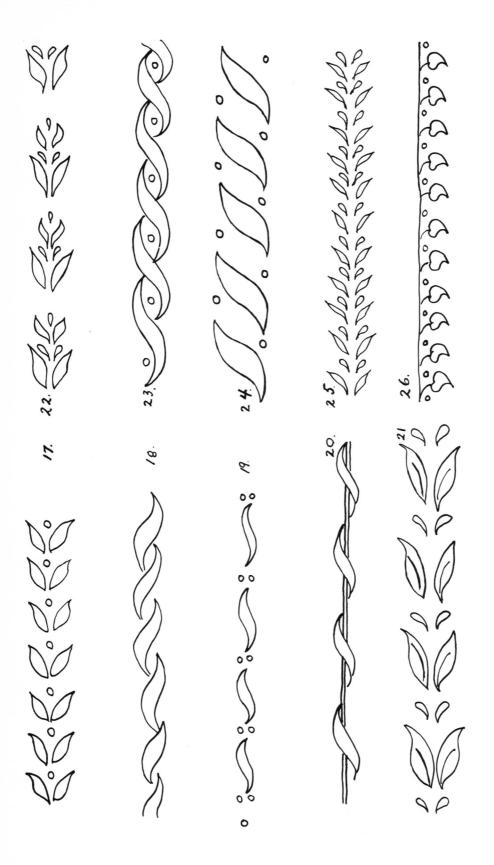

17. 18. 19. 20. 21. 22. 23. 24. 25. 26.

BRUSH STROKE BORDER PATTERNS — POINTED STROKES

Brush stroke border patterns

Rounded Strokes (p. 35)

These patterns or patterns like them are found on nearly every piece of New England country tin and on a good many Pennsylvania German pieces. Most of them derive from tinware—everything from cake boxes to document boxes and trays—in the Essex Institute in Salem, Massachusetts, and the museum of the Society for the Preservation of New England Antiquities in Boston. A few of the daintier ones have been enlarged from designs on English china of the 18th century, chiefly Worcester. You may use them as the sole trim on small pieces or as additional trim around the top or bottom of pieces decorated with large peasant motifs. 1, 2, 4, 5, 8, 9, 10, 11, 12, and 16 were originally painted in the old transparent yellow on either black or asphaltum backgrounds. 4, 6, 7, and 13 were predominantly green with red touches.

Many of these patterns would be equally suitable in gold on more formal pieces, particularly numbers 6, 7, 13, 14, 15, and 16.

Pointed Strokes (p. 36)

These pointed patterns, which require a bit greater facility with a brush to achieve a feeling of rhythm, especially in the chain or wave designs, are in general found on the same type of piece as above. 19, 22, and 23 were painted in yellow with vermilion dots, 22 in alternating pairs of red and green strokes. 21 has green leaves veined with yellow with small red strokes, on a white band. 26 is a pattern from porcelain, as is 17.

Any of the chain patterns are attractive painted in one color and shaded with a darker tone, or in gold shaded with burnt umber or burnt sienna.

Use your imagination, and these patterns will be a key to charming trims for many of your pieces.

continuous line. This seems difficult to do at first without making a double line, but success will come with practice. Practice swirls, vine tendrils, short curved lines, tiny circles, and minute dots, always using a *very tight grip* on the brush.

Tendrils and fine lines add great interest and charm to designs, so take time to learn to do them well, and with ease. A bulky stem or a crooked line will mar a pattern otherwise beautifully painted—so *practice*! Memories of the Palmer method of penmanship will be most helpful to you, if you are of that era.

IV. Stripes

This comes under a separate heading from line painting because an entirely different technique is required. Use a striping brush with soft hairs from ¾" to 1½" long, with a short quill handle, unmounted, or a "sword striper." Draw a line with silver pencil, by bracing the top joint of your fourth and little fingers on the edge of the surface and holding the pencil rather flat, drawing your hand along the edge. Wet the pencil from time to time if it does not mark well. Lay the long hairs of the striping brush flat in a mixture of color and medium, or powder and medium, and try drawing it out flat on a piece of paper. Hold the brush between your thumb and first two fingers and brace your little finger along the outside of the piece to be painted, as you draw it steadily along in a clockwise direction. Before the paint becomes noticeably thin, lay the brush in the paint again, make another practice stroke, and overlap the brush on the stripe where you left off striping last. If necessary to turn a sharp corner with the striping brush, end the stripe by raising the brush to its tip at the end of one line, and start around the corner afresh. Practice ending a line neatly on paper several times first.

For a broad stripe, draw a double line with the silver pencil.

First paint inside one line all the way, then inside the other, and fill the gap with a third overlapping row of striping before the outer stripes dry. Some artists use a broad sword striper for this purpose: its hairs are cut off diagonally so that it may be raised to a point when required.

Stripes are sometimes used around the floor of a tray as well as on the outer edge. There may be several stripes, of varying widths. A narrow stripe on the floor of a tray often accompanies a wide one at the edge. Stripes on the edge of the tray border should extend over the edge at least an eighth of an inch. Stripes need not be all the same color. They are often used to bring out two colors in the design. (See *Colors for striping*, pp. 52–53.)

Striping should be done on a varnished and well-rubbed surface in order to make a smooth stripe with a brush. It is also sometimes done with a ball-tipped drawing pen and a raised ruler, using Crowell's gold ink, Speedball yellow ink, or other special water- and varnishproof ink. In general it is best to use a brush. A very mechanical method of striping for straight edges is to place a narrow strip of masking tape on either side of the area to be striped and to draw the brush along between the two strips. This, of course, will not take care of rounded corners, so you may as well learn to stripe without such aids.

V. *Filling in a traced pattern*

When you have practiced rounded and pointed brush strokes and fine curving lines, copy a design onto tracing paper. Fasten this to a piece of firm cardboard with masking tape. Using the exact colors you will use on a real object, begin to fill in the pattern. Paint all motifs of the same color at the same time. If one brush stroke will not fill a motif of the pattern, each stroke of the brush should follow the curve of the motif as you fill it in. Do not use straight strokes on a curved motif. A large enough brush will sometimes do the job in one generous stroke, where a small brush would take several.

Allow the motifs of one color to dry before filling in others near them. (It is all too easy to rest one's hand in the work just completed.) Apply another coat when this is completely dry (after at least 24 hours), if necessary. Paint motifs of each color successively, as above, painting leaves which surround the design last. Paint the little details on the fruit or flowers, such as strawberry seeds and center stamens on flowers. Finally, embellish the design with the vine tendrils, the fine stems, the yellow, brown, or paler green veins and twisted edges seen on leaves in early designs, and the little yellow dots.

When you have thus done a pattern to your own satisfaction, paint the same pattern on a tray, a box, a chair, or whatever you choose, using your colored paper pattern as a guide.

Later, when you are using patterns you value highly, you may want to paint your sample patterns on acetate, which is a very smooth, semitransparent material, and is easier to paint on than tracing paper.

Red, green, and yellow design from a tin coffeepot

Paint this design on a black or asphaltum background. Using a #4 square-tipped brush, paint the fruit (4) with very smooth strokes in cadmium red light. Dry and apply a second coat.

Paint all brush strokes marked 2 in white, using a #3 or #4 brush according to size of stroke. Paint all brush strokes marked 3 chrome yellow with a little raw umber added. Paint fine lines in the same with a # 1 brush. Dry. 4 is done in alizarin crimson with a little burnt umber. Dry.

Now finish the design with green brush strokes and paint the calyx of the fruit dull olive green, using oxide of chrome green with raw umber and a little white.

The border trims are in the same green, but might show up better if done in yellow.

Courtesy of Society for Preservation of
New England Antiquities, Boston, Mass.

RED, GREEN, AND YELLOW DESIGN FROM A TIN COFFEEPOT

Fine brushwork on an early toleware teapot

This teapot, on exhibit in the museum of the Society for the Preservation of New England Antiquities, is one of the most perfect examples of craftsmanship in peasant style that I have seen. This design is simple but perfectly executed and well-suited to its space. The teapot is shown on page 44.

The background is black. Follow the directions for preparing, painting, and varnishing of tin, pages 11–14, 16–19.

The large round fruit is painted cadmium red. When it is completely dry, all the rounded brush strokes on the right side of the fruit are painted with a mixture of cadmium red with alizarin crimson (deep red). The largest rounded stroke on the left is also painted this deep red. The remaining five brush strokes on the left are done in white, which is left somewhat transparent (no need to give it two coats to make it opaque). When completely dry, outline the two largest deep red rounded brush strokes with a fine line of white.

The two pointed strokes surrounding the fruit are dark oxide of chromium green, as are the heart-shaped calyx and the two leaves emerging from the tip of the fruit. Some raw umber is probably used in the green. The stem line of the outer oval of leaves is yellow; all leaves inside the oval are chrome yellow. All leaves (brush strokes) outside the oval are dark oxide of chromium green.

The wave pattern trimming the piece is done with consecutive brush strokes in solid yellow (not a chain line pattern). Two very fine lines in chrome yellow trim either side of the wave pattern. Two similar lines run around the top of the pot.

The lid is decorated with the same solid wave pattern in chrome yellow, with tiny cadmium red dots to enliven it. Yellow brush strokes surround the top handle.

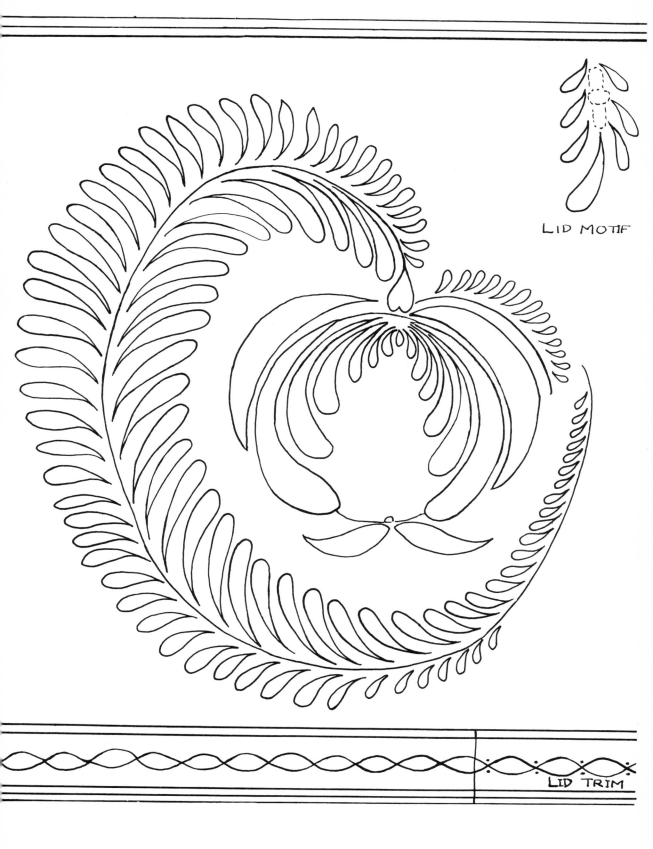

LID MOTIF

LID TRIM

FINE BRUSHWORK ON AN EARLY TOLEWARE TEAPOT

THREE TYPICAL PIECES OF NEW ENGLAND COUNTRY TINWARE

A MOLASSES PITCHER, DOCUMENT BOX, AND TEAPOT, DECORATED WITH SIMPLE BRUSH STROKES 1800 – 1825

Society for Preservation of
New England Antiquities, Boston, Mass.

C H A P T E R 5

Colors

I. *Basic list of artist's oil colors for beginners*

With the following list, you will be able to mix most of the colors needed for primitive designs. Later you will wish to add others for specific uses.

American vermilion
Cadmium yellow medium
Prussian blue
Yellow ochre
Raw umber
Burnt umber
Drop black or ivory black
Titanium or flake white (large tube)

For transparent coats of color, you will also need alizarin crimson and yellow lake. Alizarin crimson is also useful in toning reds.

White is added to most colors. It is often needed to make them more opaque. If a color is too bright, add either a touch of raw

EIGHTEENTH-CENTURY PENNSYLVANIA CHEST

PENNSYLVANIA GERMAN
SGRAFFITO PLATE

Metropolitan Museum of Art, New York

umber (used most with the cool colors) or a touch of its complementary color. Burnt umber is added to the warm colors to take the edge off their brightness and to give them a mellow tone.

II. *How to mix a variety of colors*

You will find that this list sometimes calls for colors you do not have in your beginner's set. You may, however, use it as a guide. If you find you are not satisfied with the exact color you are getting, adding one of the colors mentioned may make the difference.

Blues:
> Clear light blue: Prussian blue * and white
> Dull blue: white and Prussian blue, touch of raw umber
> Gray-blue: same, with more white
> Green-blue: same as dull blue, plus extra white and touch of chrome yellow medium or cadmium yellow medium
> Cold slate blue: Prussian blue, white, lampblack
> Turquoise: Prussian blue, chrome green, white, raw umber

Yellows:
> Clear yellow: cadmium yellow medium plus white
> Corn yellow: chrome yellow plus white
> "Country yellow," or "old yellow": chrome yellow, yellow ochre, white, and a touch of raw umber
> Mustard yellow: chrome yellow, Prussian blue, white, touch of raw umber (greenish cast) ; *or*
> chrome yellow, touch of raw umber and a touch of chrome green, white
> Citron yellow: chrome yellow plus white, a touch of Prussian blue
> Clear light yellow: cadmium yellow light, white, and a touch of vermilion

Greens:
> Light green for leaves: chrome green light, Phillips white, touch of raw umber

* Prussian blue is very strong. Use tiny amounts.

Gray-green for leaves: cadmium yellow medium; *or*
> chrome yellow medium, Prussian blue, white, raw umber;
> *or*
> chrome green medium, white, raw umber

Olive green: oxide of chromium, white, raw umber

Yellow-green: chrome green medium, white, cadmium yellow
> light, raw umber; *or*
> cadmium yellow medium, a touch of Prussian blue, white,
> raw umber

Blue-green: cadmium yellow medium or
> chrome green medium, Prussian blue, a little white, a
> touch of raw umber

Dark green: chrome green dark, drop black and a little white;
> *or*
> Prussian blue, cadmium yellow medium, drop black, white

Dark blue-green: chrome green medium, Prussian blue, plenty
> of black, white

Chartreuse: chrome yellow, Prussian blue, raw umber

Citron: lemon yellow, Prussian blue, raw umber, white

Reds:

Brick red: Venetian or Indian red

Orange red: American vermilion

Light bright red: cadmium red light

Deep red: alizarin crimson, cadmium red light, white, and
> burnt umber; *or*
> alizarin crimson, American vermilion, white, and raw
> umber

Bright cherry red (for bright fruit): cadmium red light and
> alizarin crimson

Deeper red (with which to make shadows on the cherry-red
> fruit): alizarin crimson and raw sienna

Violets:

Cool violet: ultramarine blue, alizarin crimson, raw umber,
> white

Warm violet: mauve

Browns:
 Beige: yellow ochre, white, burnt umber, touch of vermilion
 Dull brown: raw sienna, white
 Red-brown: burnt sienna; *or*
  burnt sienna with raw umber
 Warm dark brown: Vandyke brown
 Transparent brown for shading gold designs: burnt umber

Grays:
 Warm gray: white, raw umber, touch of vermilion
 Cold blue-gray: white, Prussian blue, lampblack
 Greenish-gray: white, raw umber, touch·of chrome green medium or oxide of chromium
 Dove gray: white, raw umber, Prussian blue; *or*
  Payne's gray, or neutral

Off-whites:
 Oyster white: white, raw umber
 Ivory: white, yellow ochre, raw umber (vermilion optional)
 Cool white: white plus a touch of cobalt blue

Pinks:
 Rose pink: cadmium red light, white, alizarin crimson; *or*
  alizarin crimson, yellow ochre, white, raw umber
 Warm pink: cadmium red light, white, burnt sienna
 Coral: cadmium red light, white, cadmium orange, burnt sienna
 Dusty rose: white, Venetian red, touch of green
 Flesh: American vermilion, yellow ochre, white

III. *Characteristics of certain artist's oil colors*

When you are thoroughly familiar with the basic colors and are acquainted with the results of mixing them, you may wish to add other useful ones. The characteristics of a number of them follow:

 Alizarin crimson: pure deep wine red, used for transparent washes on flowers and fruit and in mixing cool rose, red, and violet

American vermilion: light strong red, used alone and in orange, brown, and beige

Burnt sienna: reddish brown used in shading over gold, ivory, and the like, in mixing warm pinks and corals, and in antiquing

Burnt umber: transparent brown used for shading, particularly over gold; used in antiquing, sometimes combined with burnt sienna; used to mix deep transparent reds combined with alizarin

Cadmium red light: very bright light red used alone and for mixing rose, red, and orange

Cadmium red medium: deep red with a wine cast

Cadmium red deep: very dark "solid" red

Cadmium yellow light: clear light yellow

Cadmium yellow medium: light butter yellow

Cadmium yellow deep: deep butter yellow

Cadmium orange: strong, garish orange

Chrome green light #1: bright bud green

Chrome green medium #2: grass green, good for mixing many greens

Chrome green medium #3: dark green, sometimes tinged with blue; good for mixing dark leaf greens and background shades of dark green and blue-green

Chrome oxide green: dark olive green, excellent for copying leaf color used in English and early American toleware painting

Crimson lake: deep pinkish red, transparent

Emerald green: brilliant green, good for mixing with yellows

English vermilion: light mellow red, better than American vermilion for toleware painting

Gamboge: semitransparent golden yellow, used over bronzes and used with Prussian blue to make a transparent green

Indian red: rust or brick red

Indian yellow: semitransparent yellow

King's yellow: strong buttercup yellow

Mauve: pinkish violet

Neutral: soft warm gray

Payne's gray: good medium gray

Permanent green: bright green

Prussian blue: deep transparent clear blue, used in mixing greens, turquoise, and dull blue; also as a transparent wash over silver and gold. Do not use with zinc white, as chemical darkening takes place.

Raw sienna: dull golden brown, used in mixing browns and tans

Raw umber: brownish-black, nearly always used to dull other colors

Ultramarine blue: pure deep cold blue, used in mixing cool violets and purple

Vandyke brown: warm dark brown, darkens chemically with age

Venetian red: brick color

Verdigris: blue-green, transparent

Yellow lake: transparent yellow for washes over gold, light colors, and for mixing transparent greens

Yellow ochre: muddy yellow, much used in old yellows; also used for mixing ivory, beige, and creamy yellows

Whites:

Phillips white: very opaque, chemically stable, keeps well

Permalba: same

Titanium white: same

Cremnitz white and flake white: used in glass painting; does not spread excessively

Black:

Drop black: "warm" black, good for tinting colors with white bases, such as pearl gray, warm olive, and so forth

Ivory black: same as above, made from better-grade bone

Lampblack: used in making dark shades of colors, when cold tone is desired as in slate blue, steel gray, and so forth

IV. *Colors for peasant decoration*

Red flowers: vermilion with raw umber

Blue flowers: Prussian blue with raw umber

Yellow flowers: yellow ochre

Red fruit: cadmium red light and alizarin crimson

Shadows on same: dark red: alizarin crimson with raw sienna or burnt umber

Details on red fruit: white or yellow

Highlights on dark red fruit: white, yellow, or light red

Highlights on light red fruit: white or yellow

Yellow fruit: chrome yellow, yellow ochre, white, and touch of raw umber

Shadows or details on same: yellow ochre, or yellow ochre with a little burnt sienna; or burnt umber alone

Gray-green leaves: chrome green medium with white and raw umber

Veins on gray-green leaves: black

Olive-green leaves: oxide of chrome green white, raw umber

Very dark green leaves: Prussian blue, raw sienna, and raw umber

Veins on dark green leaves: yellow or white

Leaf tips on same: yellow or white

Reddish leaves: Venetian red or other earth color

Transparent brown leaves, or scrollwork: burnt umber with burnt sienna

The above colors are frequently seen in peasant painting, but you may not wish to follow the originals so closely. Color in modern Swedish peasant painting is clearer and bolder than in old Pennsylvania Dutch (German) decoration. The Swedes use more red, yellow, and blue, with some green and white. The blue is Prussian blue with white, the green as above, the yellow chrome yellow with white, the red American vermilion or cadmium red light. All these colors may be toned down to be more harmonious.

V. Colors for striping

Striping adds so much life to most painted articles that it is well to be familiar with good combinations of color for striping.

Background color	Striping color
Old yellow	Reddish brown: burnt sienna
	Dark brown: burnt umber with raw umber; *or* burnt umber alone

Black: ivory or drop black
Green: chrome green, white, and raw umber; *or*
    Prussian blue, chrome yellow, white, and raw
    umber; *or*
    oxide of chromium green, white, and raw
    umber
In case two stripes are desired, use:
    reddish brown and black, *or*
    dark brown and black, *or*
    green and black.

Pale yellow	Vermilion Dark green

Black	White
	Old yellow: chrome yellow and burnt umber; *or*
	    chrome yellow, white, and raw umber
	Gold or silver bronze, if to harmonize with a
	    bronze center design

Gray	Dull blue American vermilion
Vermilion	Black Yellow Gold bronze or gold leaf
Ivory	Reddish brown: burnt sienna and burnt umber Brown: burnt umber Gold bronze or gold leaf
Venetian red	White
Dark green	Pale yellow: chrome yellow, white, raw umber
Pale green	Black Vermilion Deep blue Gold bronze or gold leaf
Light blue	Deep blue: Prussian blue, raw umber, white
Old rose	Dull blue: Prussian blue, raw umber
Lavender	Deep blue-green: chrome green, Prussian blue, white, raw umber

Early New England Design for Cut Corner Tray (Reversible)

Early New England design for cut-corner tray (reversible)

This design is done in pure bright colors on a dark background such as dark green or black. The pattern shown is turned around and painted on the other half of the tray as well.

1. Cherries and centers of "tulips" are cadmium red light or vermilion with a touch of raw umber; two coats. Stylized shadows alizarin crimson with touch of burnt umber. Dotted highlights white.

2. Petaled flowers slightly deeper shade of red. Add a touch of alizarin crimson to above. Two coats. Shadows alizarin crimson with a touch of burnt umber.

3. "Tulips," lower leaves and stems, and brush strokes at left of design: first coat white, second country yellow. Shadows are mixture of burnt umber and burnt sienna.

4. Leaves (except those at top) and brush strokes are light medium green, one or two coats. Accents light gray-green.

5. Top young leaves may be yellowish bud green, or same as others. Accents yellow.

6. Border strokes and stripe, old yellow. Stripe on edge, same.

7. Give the entire tray, when dry, a coat of varnish with a little burnt umber in it. Dry. Rub down. Follow directions for finishing, pages 159–160.

Border Designs from Old Tinware

Border designs from old tinware

1. Design in green on a transparent white band one and a half inches wide. Small details are cadmium red light. Background of document box on which it was found was asphaltum.

2. Running flower and leaf pattern, from a copper luster pitcher. Design in gold on a blue band. (Asphaltum duplicates the copper luster color nicely on tin.)

3. Brush strokes on white band are green. The flower is red with a yellow center.

4. Green leaves, red berries, and red flower on transparent white band. Center of flower is deeper red.

5. Swedish border pattern. Leaves may be painted gray-green, the daisy two shades of blue, the spotted flower two shades of terra cotta (Venetian red plus white).

6. Another pattern from a document box. Green strokes on transparent white band, dots red. Background of box black.

7. Transparent yellow brush stroke design from a New England "cut corner" tray. Dark background.

8. Pattern from the border of a sixteenth-century Syrian tile.

Suggested colors: Gray-green intertwining stems. Leaves graded shades of green, from gray-green dark to gray-green light. Flowers alternately blue and rose. (Shade the blue flowers from dark to light; the rose flowers from brick red to dusty pink.) Tip scalloped edges with white.

It is interesting to note the similarity of this design to the modern Swedish patterns. Peasant art forms seem to repeat although streams of origin may be widely divergent.

Border designs from old tinware, continued

9. *Leaves are dark oxide of chrome green, transparent yellow touches of color on them. Small leaves are yellow; small bud yellow. Stems and lines on middle fruit of group, black.*

10. *Fruit design from a cake box (New England). The fruit is red with white highlights, painted on a white band. The small leaf and the part of the fruit which attaches it to the stem are yellow. All lines are black, as is the background of the box itself.*

11. *This design (from a document box) is particularly curving and graceful. Again, it is applied on a semitransparent white band over a black background. The oxide of chrome green leaves have yellow tips. Yellow is used as highlight on the cadmium red (light) "cherries." The lines—stems and the like—are black. The border below was found on same box.*

12. *This design was painted directly on the black background of the box above and shares the fluid lines of its accompanying border.*

The flowers are cadmium red (light) with yellow dots, the leaves the same green, and the little hanging buds white except for the part that attaches them to the stem, which is red. Stems are black.

PAINTED DESIGN FOR TOP OF A
COUNTRY CHAIR

Painted design for top of a country chair

Background: very deep brown flat paint, to be followed by coat of varnish when dry.

Paint background of large leaf pale yellow-green. When dry, shade leaf near base and along center rib with transparent coat of burnt umber with medium. Let dry 12 hours. Paint strokes around edge of leaf in olive green, slightly overlapping each other. When dry, paint small cream brush strokes along upper highlighted edge of leaf, just inside olive-green strokes. Paint veins and ovals black when this dries, with finest brush. When dry, fill ovals with off-white.

Paint grapes light olive-green. When dry, paint underside of grapes with oxide of chrome green mixed with white and burnt umber, and shade to lighter color until pale yellow highlight is reached, as you paint upward. When thoroughly dry, add small black curved lines.

Paint wheat stems olive green. Wheat grains are olive green, highlighted in corn yellow on upper side. Sharp tiny black lines emphasize the underside of each grain. Sprays around grains are corn yellow. The largest stems of wheat are olive green tipped in yellow white. Fine curly lines are yellow white.

The design is bordered with a corn-yellow stripe.

Flowing pattern from an early New England cake tin

This decorated a large round tin box with a hinged lid. The background was asphaltum in varnish, which gives a copper effect. The large design was on the front; the cherry border pattern above it on a semitransparent white band. This only went halfway around. The trim circled the sides of the lid, and there was a small circular pattern on the top. The principal pattern might be changed to suit almost any shape. The curving yellow tendrils add to its grace.

Paint the background black, or use asphaltum as described in Chapter 10. Varnish and rub down as directed there.

Dip a #4 square-tipped brush into varnish, then pick up a little white oil color on the brush. Stroke out a little on paper and brush onto the border in long smooth strokes, making a semitransparent, but not streaked, white background for the cherry pattern. When dry, varnish over this and rub down.

Paint the cherries, and the fruit and flowers in the main design (1), in cadmium red light with a #3 or #4 brush, in smooth strokes. Dry. Give a second coat of red. Dry. Paint all brush strokes on the fruit and flowers marked 2 in white, using #3 quill brush. Dry. (One coat will suffice.) Now paint brush strokes marked 3 in burnt umber, with a touch of alizarin crimson added. Dry. All remaining leaves (4) are a dull olive-green. Oxide of green with raw umber added is the best mixture for this.

When dry, paint in all the remaining brush strokes in chrome yellow medium with a touch of raw umber added. Use a scroller for the yellow lines which surround the design.

Paint the brush strokes on the sides of the lid with a #4 square-tipped or pointed quill brush. Use #2 brush for the smaller strokes on top, using yellow above.

Courtesy of Society for Preservation of New England Antiquities, Boston, Mass.

62

FLOWING PATTERN FROM AN EARLY NEW ENGLAND CAKE TIN

Fancy Sheraton Chair with Brush Stroke Painting

Essex Institute, Salem, Mass.

6

The use of bronze powders in painting and freehand bronzing

There is a wide variety of bronze powders on the market, even in gold shades alone. Powders must be very finely ground if you do not wish them to resemble radiator paint. Coarse bronze will quickly drop off the sides of a jar or tube when you shake it; fine powder will cling to the glass. Most makers indicate increasing fineness by higher code numbers. The color of a bronze powder can be best judged by actual use on a dark background. If this is not possible, judge it by its appearance through the outside of the glass, rather than by its appearance as you look down inside the jar. A little rubbed on your finger will sometimes be a help in judging the color.

The following, in a very fine grind, will take care of most stenciling, painting with bronze, or freehand bronzing.

Pale gold lining, such as Venus #57, sometimes called lemon
   gold
Brushed brass or rich gold
Deep gold (orange colored)
Chromium, nontarnishing, or aluminum, a softer color
Brilliant fire, for highlights on fruit and the like
Copper or antique copper

The powders may be combined for gradual shading from one color to another, or for new colors. Silver-colored bronze is often mixed with gold to get a burnished effect in fruit. Brilliant fire, mixed with copper or antique copper, gives a softly glowing copper color.

In general, the pure colors, such as blue, green, and red, should not be used in powder form, but should be made by adding a little transparent oil color to a varnish coat over gold or silver. If you do use the colored bronzes, blue, green, or red, mix them with gold or silver for a mellow effect.

I. Painting with bronze powders

Materials: #1 and #3 pointed quill brushes
Medium (half turpentine, half spar varnish)
Bronze powders, in a fine grade which will adhere to
   the sides of a glass jar
Palette: a piece of glass, a slick magazine, or piece
   of cardboard wrapped in heavy waxed paper
Palette knife
Jar lids, to hold bronze powders
Turpentine and paint cloths

Trace your design onto the painted article and prepare your materials as described in Chapter 2. Put a tiny heap of bronze powder of the desired color, whether silver, gold, or brilliant fire, on a flat tin lid. Have ready a bottle cap or oil cup containing the medium, as well as a small jar of turpentine. Dip the tip of a #3 pointed quill brush into the medium, as described for painting a design in the previous chapter. Then pick up a little bronze powder on the end of the wet brush. Draw the brush out on paper a little to see that it is smoothly filled. Then paint in the design with brush strokes, using a finer brush where fine lines make it necessary.

When each bronze-painted motif is almost dry—when a finger applied to it feels only the slightest adhesion—take a sable square-tipped brush, dip it dry into bronze powder, and brush it onto the design while tacky. Watch the fine lines closely, as they dry rapidly. This extra surface coat of bronze, when done in gold, resembles gold leaf. (Some painters use a coat of vermilion oil color, mixed with medium, before brushing on the bronze, instead of painting with bronze and medium.)

If the design uses two or more shades of bronze powder, as in a leaf pattern where variation is needed, use the different bronzes on different days, as loose grains of bronze may adhere where they are not wanted, on sticky surfaces.

When the work has dried for 24 hours, use a feather duster or a very soft cloth to dust off loose gold. Wash with soap and water carefully to remove any surplus gold from the background.

Any errors outside the pattern must be covered up with background color.

Gold designs are usually given third-dimensional feeling by shadows of semitransparent brown-toned oil colors applied with medium. Burnt umber, or burnt sienna combined with burnt umber, may be used. Sometimes Prussian blue is combined with yellow lake or gamboge to make shadows of a yellow-green color, but this is not usual. Apply the color a little more heavily on the side most deeply shadowed to give a feeling of depth.

The veins on leaves may be painted with a very fine scroller brush, using burnt umber, drop black, or whatever color is most appropriate. Veins are sometimes drawn in with croquille pen and India ink in fine designs. Details surrounding the gold design are sometimes drawn with pen and white, gold, or red waterproof ink.

BELLOWS DECORATED
IN FREEHAND BRONZE

Bellows decorated in freehand bronze

1. *Paint background country yellow, using two or three coats.*

2. *Trace the fruit onto the bellows with graphite paper. Paint grapes, apple, quince, and pear with a mixture of flat black paint and varnish, or with black Serviceseal. The small grapes will dry quickly, so treat them with bronze first. As soon as the black coat reaches the tacky stage, apply rich gold bronze powder with a piece of velvet or chamois, or with a soft brush as described on page 71. Polish the highlights on the grapes solidly. The gold fades out as it approaches the dark areas indicated. Allow a very thin rim of black to mark the edges of the grapes. When the finish on large fruit has also reached the tacky stage, polish the main highlight areas with rich gold. As the brightness fades out toward the thin dark rim and toward the shadows, pick up a very little brilliant fire bronze to mix with the gold on the same piece of velvet. Apply the mixed powders there to give a faint natural blush to the fruit. The blossom end of the fruit is treated with gold alone.*

Varnish the piece after allowing the previous work to dry for 24 hours. Rub down. Dry.

3. *Trace onto bellows all leaves around central group and leaves on handle. Paint the large leaves surrounding the fruit except group at lower left, and paint those on the handle in black as above. Brush the tips with brilliant fire powder and blend gold over the rest of the leaves. If you touch the edges brightly with gold and leave much of the leaf in shadow it will have an effect of curving and depth. (The veins are subsequently painted in black.) For the lower left group of fruit leaves, paint black at same time as leaves mentioned above. Apply brilliant fire powder around edges. Cut a small bit of architect's linen in a convex curve and lay it wherever veins are desired, applying powder next to the linen's edge. (Leave the center area dark, of course, when applying the brilliant fire bronze.)*

4. *Leaves of border: Paint leaves black. Brush brilliant fire on tips of leaves. Apply rich gold bronze as under (4) for veining. Leave center vein area dark; it will be painted in.*

5. *Paint stems between fruit black and powder with gold, except edges.*

6. *Varnish all.*

7. *Painted details of large leaves and fruit: Paint veins of (4) leaves with #1 pointed quill brush, using black oil color mixed with medium.*

69

Bellows decorated in freehand bronze, continued

Paint veins of (6) leaves in black, somewhat diluted, cross-hatching the center vein.

Paint details of blossom end of pear and quince in burnt umber with medium. Paint center shadows of flower on handle in burnt umber also.

8. Border flowers: Paint flowers with a mixture of lemon gold (pale gold) bronze and medium, enough to cover well. Apply gold leaf to this area when almost dry, following the directions in Chapter 7. When this has been dry a short while, etch the fine lines shown with a sharp tool, as described in the same chapter.

If you prefer not to use gold leaf, powder over the area when almost dry with dry gold bronze powder. In this case, details are painted in black.

9. Varnish the piece after 24 hours. (Gold leaf is very susceptible to damage until varnished.)

10. Final details: Paint stamens and anthers (and fine lines in flowers if not etched), all fine black lines, and small leaves in black oil color mixed with medium. Trim the bellows with a fine black line very near the edge.

11. Finishing: Follow directions in Chapter 10.

II. *Freehand bronzing on painted motifs*

Materials: Black Serviceseal, or flat black paint with varnish
Soft round-tipped brush or piece of chamois or
firm velvet (heavy silk millinery velvet is best)
Paper towels or soft cloth

The effect of freehand bronzing is similar to stenciling, but is in general somewhat softer and less sharply outlined. It is often combined with painting in the same design. Its effect is best against a light background. If the background is dark, you may paint a light band on which to apply the bronzed motifs.

Paint the parts to be bronzed—leaves or fruit, for example—with the Serviceseal or paint-varnish mix. (Black Serviceseal is a paint generally sold for painting wire screens.) While it is drying, put a very little fine bronze powder on a porous surface such as a cloth or absorbent paper. When the black paint is just tacky, press the brush, velvet, or chamois lightly into the bronze on the absorbent material, then against the clean absorbent material itself to remove surplus. Apply it with a circular motion from the brightest highlight outward, making it fade to nothing as it approaches the shadows.

On leaves, the powder is applied sharply at the very edge, but fades to nothing in the hollows of the leaf. Fruits are highly polished on the foremost round parts, and the edge is marked in bronze. Highest highlights may be touched with brilliant fire bronze to represent the blush of the fruit. (The entire fruit may have a coat of transparent alizarin crimson, instead of the brilliant fire bronze, if desired, when dry. In this case, the whole fruit may be powdered again in gold for the highlights, the shadows remaining crimson.)

Flowers are usually brushed with bronze at the outer edges, fading into shadow near their deepest center. The brush is used very lightly in bronzing flower petals or leaves, and more heavily on solid forms such as fruit.

Leaves of olive or gray-green, powdered lightly with gold or silver, and veined in transparent umber, are charming with this type of freehand bronze. Different flowers may be colored in different shades of bronze to give variety. Leaves are sometimes bronzed in part copper and part silver on top of a gold border. The technique is suitable for both modern and antique reproduction work.

If any painted details are added over the freehand bronzing, apply a varnish coat first and rub it down.

Fine border designs

1. Gold border originally painted on a vermilion champagne cooler. The large motifs are applied in pale gold leaf, etched with fine lines. The small leaves and the fine lines are painted with pale gold lining bronze and powdered with the same while tacky. It was accompanied by a stripe of chrome yellow. (Harrison Gray Otis House, Boston, Mass.)

2. A charming gold border of leaves and tendrils, applied in gold leaf on a black background. The veins are etched with a sharp tool. The vines and tendrils may be applied with a croquille pen and waterproof, varnishproof gold ink, or painted in gold bronze with a #1 pointed quill brush, or a scroller brush. (See line work, *p. 34.)*

I have seen this same pattern charmingly painted in color. The leaves were soft gray-green, dusted with gold powder, and strawberries of gold, tinted with transparent crimson, took the place of some of the leaves. The strawberries had fine seeds of burnt umber and yellow. Tendrils and so forth were gold.

3. This is the border also seen on the bellows painted and freehand bronzed, illustrated on page 68.

The leaves and flowers may be painted with gold bronze or applied in gold leaf. Or they may, especially on a light background, be first painted in black Serviceseal (see freehand bronzing, *pp. 70–71) and brushed with bronze. The fine lines and small leaves may be painted with a fine brush or done with a pen and varnishproof ink. (Essex Institute, Salem, Mass.)*

4. This somewhat over-fancy leaf design was originally used on a tray which had a center group of roses. It might well be used alone.

The background may either be black or pastel. The leaves are soft gray-green. When the green is nearly dry, brush on silver bronze from the outside edges toward the center, leaving the center area clear. After varnishing and rubbing with pumice, paint the veins and curlicues in "old yellow," using a scroller or #1 pointed quill brush. The tiny flowers are white with vermilion or yellow centers, or may be painted any color that ties in with the background.

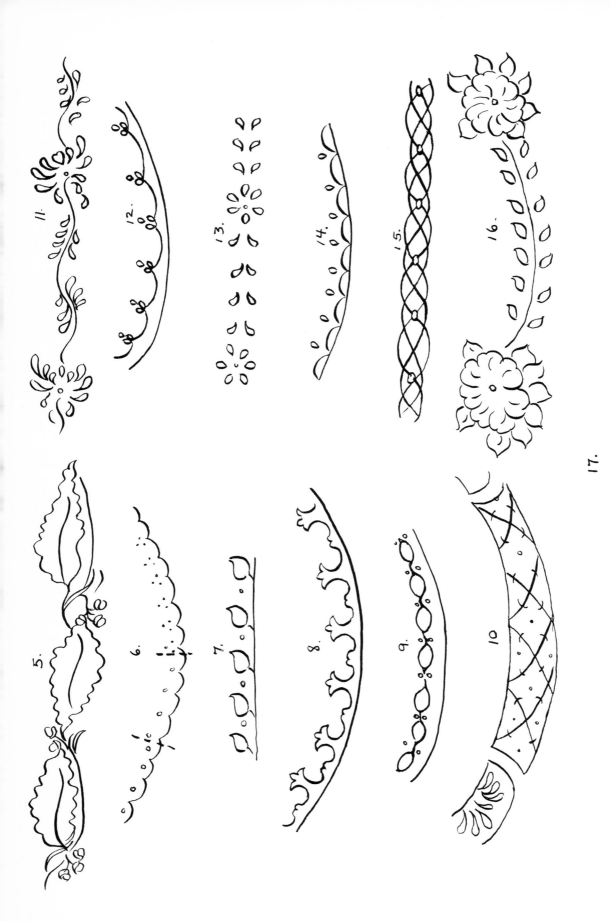

5.

6.

7.

8.

9.

10.

11.

12.

13.

14.

15.

16.

17.

Fine border designs, continued

These designs (5–17) are largely from 18th-century china, with the exception of 15. This design of interwoven lines is often seen on the so-called sandwich trays (rectangular trays with rounded corners and hand-holes). It is usually painted on a wide solid gold band, the tray itself being black or orange-red. The lines are white and red or white and black.

The design runs only along the sides and the ends, not around the corners. These are painted with a special motif of their own, often resembling a shell. There is usually a stripe of white and a stripe of red on the gold band.

III. *The use of pen and ink or brush for detail work over bronze*

Materials: #0, #00, or #1 pointed quill brush
Artist's oil colors
Varnish
or
Crow-quill pen
Waterproof, varnishproof ink

Very fine lines are often used on delicate gold patterns. They are used as veins in leaves or lines radiating from the center of a flower, or the shadow and detail lines on a shell—all calling for delicate work difficult to achieve with a brush. They may be painted with the tiniest of brushes dipped in a mixture of artist's oil colors and varnish (no turpentine for this). Or you may work with a crow-quill pen and waterproof, varnishproof India ink. Apply the desired pattern with this fine penpoint *after* the gold work has had a protective varnish coat applied, and has been rubbed with pumice and water.

IV. Colored inks in decorating

Materials: Crow-quill pen and holder

Waterproof, varnishproof colored inks

A variety of colored and metallic inks is available which challenges the imagination to provide uses in original decorating. Some flow more smoothly than others, so test a new ink over a varnished surface before using to see if it will work properly for this purpose.

Black, yellow, white, and red inks are those most often used. They are applied with a crow-quill pen. Black and yellow inks are suitable in old designs for making fine tendrils, veins, leaves, dots, line patterns, and stripes. White ink is used largely for fine crisscrossed lines such as those which fill the spaces in large medallion patterns. (These are often painted in gold bronze

Medallions and other baroque motifs

Rich scroll motifs such as those illustrated here may be used by themselves to decorate a tray, as a frame for a floral group, or for an elaborate monogram. They may also be used in part for corner motifs, or assembled as borders.

They are more suited to a formal piece than a homely one, and would never be combined with a peasant design.

Gold is therefore the natural medium for them, although several tints and shades of a color may make an equally decorative treatment, especially on furniture. Gold is sometimes combined with white, black, or color in scrollwork of this kind. Color might be used especially for those parts such as the cross-hatching, dots, or small floral touches. Gold scrolls are often shaded with burnt umber or burnt sienna. Colored scrolls would of course be shaded in a deeper self-tone. They may be applied in gold leaf or painted in bronze.

ANY SCENIC, FLORAL, FRUIT, OR CLASSIC DESIGN MAY BE ENHANCED BY BORDERS IN THIS SPIRIT, IF RELATED PROPERLY TO STYLE AND SHAPE OF BACKGROUND.

MEDALLIONS

THE SCROLL IN BORDER FORM AND
FRAMING A FLORAL GROUP

mixed with varnish, also.) Crowell's gold ink is appropriate for this use, provided that its shade harmonizes with the other gold used in the pattern. An off shade of gold may ruin a piece of work entirely.

In working with gold or colored inks it is necessary to shake the bottle well and often as you progress, for the pigments tend to separate quickly from the ink and to settle. Trace your lines very finely and proceed as you would in painting lines.

The scroll in border form and framing a floral group

Floral group

The large floral motif was derived from a 1770 Worcester coffeepot. The medallion adorned a pea-green background and the scrollwork was largely in gold and Venetian red, or rouge-de-fer in porcelain parlance. You may use your own color scheme for the floral arrangement, or substitute for it a decorative group of fruit and flowers, or a scene of some kind. The center flower may become a rose by the judicious addition of unfolding petals, or may be a daisy type of flower with a raised center. If a rose, I would suggest making all bell-shaped flowers yellowish-white, the tulip shape at the top a deep blue, the open flowers above the rose soft blue (deep blue on the shadow side), the dark flowers beneath the rose violet, and the flowers which are dropping their petals yellow with dark cone centers. The large leaves might be done in an oxide of chrome green with dark veins, and the small leaves a little lighter. Keep the leaves very subdued in value. The little berries at the top are red.

Borders

The borders have been arranged in a straight line to conform to a rectangular page. They become really interesting, however, when appropriately curving around an oval or circular shape. Try rearranging them on your sketch pad before discarding the idea of using them on some of your curved pieces.

For colors, see the directions for medallions and baroque motifs, page 77.

Stripes may be ruled if you can obtain a ruler with a very sharp edge and a rubber backstrip which holds it slightly above the level of your work so that the ink does not spread. (An old hand at striping with a brush would throw up his hands in horror at the idea of striping with a ruler, putting such practices in a class with the use of a mechanical striping gadget found at auto supply stores.)

V. Raised flowers painted on gold borders

You will often see raised flowers in white or color as part of gold border designs. In the Victorian era these were often applied with mother-of-pearl. Raised flowers often add greatly to the beauty of a design, but are impractical on any surface receiving much use. They are most suitable on boxes or purely decorative pieces.

The raised effect may be achieved by the use of five or six coats of white enamel. This may be tinted afterward. China-type substances and plaster fillers have also been used. However, the china variety, as used in mending porcelain, has a tendency to crackle, and the plaster variety may dissolve away in washing, so paint is really the safest to apply.

The flowers may be colored with transparent oil colors or detailed in gold. Before they are painted in, a gold outline may be painted, which adds to their effectiveness.

The use of gold leaf

Gold leaf has more luster than bronze powders applied with varnish. It is somewhat difficult to handle, and expensive if used extensively, so is usually reserved for small touches, such as the centers of flowers in designs painted with bronze powders, or for very elaborate trays.

Metal leaf comes in silver as well as gold, but the silver tarnishes quickly and must be protected with varnish at once. Aluminum leaf is generally used for silver color.

I. How to purchase and handle gold leaf

Gold leaf comes in two forms. The ordinary way of buying it is in small booklets, about 3½″ square. Each leaf is between two sheets of tissue paper. It is so thin that the least movement of air will cause it to crumple, so must be handled, and the book opened, with the greatest care.

Another way of packaging it is in booklets, with each leaf already adhering to a thin sheet of paper. It is applied just as the other is. I personally prefer using the loose leaf, though it is a little more trouble to use.

To remove loose gold leaf from the book, open it to the first leaf, slowly turning back the tissue page as you open it. Do not have a door or window open and avoid breathing on the leaf, for it will crumple easily. Have ready a piece of thin waxed paper, cut to the size of the booklet. Lay it gently in place over the leaf. With the warmth of your finger, but without any vigorous rubbing, smooth over the paper until the warmth of your finger on the waxed paper makes it stick to the gold.

II. *How to apply gold leaf*

Materials: Gold or aluminum leaf on waxed paper
Fine gold or aluminum bronze powder
Varnish and turpentine medium
#1 and #3 pointed quill brushes
Absorbent cotton, or small piece of velvet

Before applying the gold leaf, paint the design in with bronze powder to match the leaf, exactly as in painting with bronze powders. (Dip your #1 or #3 brush in medium, then in dry bronze, mixing the two together; then paint.) When the painted areas feel only slightly sticky (when a finger applied leaves no mark, but barely adheres) pick up the sheet of waxed paper and gold leaf. Lay the gold leaf on the painted design, and smooth it gently over the design, using your finger or a piece of absorbent cotton or velvet. When the shape of your motif is completely showing through the waxed paper, where the gold leaf has adhered to the design, lift the paper by a corner. You will find that only the surplus gold leaf is left on the paper, which may be used for other parts of the design later. If the gold leaf has not adhered to all parts of the design, quickly relay gold leaf over the space missed, and the joint will be hardly noticeable. Do not go back over the area again until 24 hours later.

After that time, take a piece of absorbent cotton or velvet and, with utmost care, push away any little frills of extra gold leaf which have not come cleanly away with the paper from the edges of the design. Gold leaf is very easily scratched and must be carefully handled until it has a protective coat of varnish over it. Varnish is applied about 24 hours after laying the gold leaf, and is rubbed down with pumice and water 24 hours after that. If you are etching the gold leaf, delay the varnishing until that is done.

III. *Etching gold leaf*

> *Materials:* A pin vise, a tool that holds a phonograph needle

Etching is usually done freehand, as tracing would leave a heavy mark on the delicate gold leaf. No erasure is possible, of course. Sketch the desired lines in on your tracing paper for practice.

Hold the object to be etched, if a small one, firmly in your left hand. Steady the etching tool in a vertical position in your right hand. Draw it toward you with a very steady stroke. If you drag on it, it may go through the background color to the wood or metal, making a rough furrow in the leaf. Nor can you make too light a stroke, as only one stroke in one place is possible. As you become skilful with your tool, your etched lines will become neat and sure, although at first they may look as though gouged out with a burr. Experience is the only teacher for this, but success comes quickly.

There are a great many simple line patterns which may be etched into a gold leaf stripe around the edge, or on the floor of a tray. Examine the patterns shown on the page of borders (page 74). The pattern of wavy line with circlets above and below each wave (17) was etched on a gold leaf stripe only a quarter of an inch wide.

IV. *Adding details to gold leaf motifs with paints*

After a protective coat of varnish has been applied and allowed to dry, and has been rubbed with pumice and water, details may be painted in if the etching process has not been used, or in addition to etching.

> *Materials:* #1 and #3 pointed quill brushes
> Medium (varnish and turpentine mixture)
> Transparent oil colors, such as burnt umber
> Ivory black oil color, Burnt sienna

Shadows on leaves and baroque motifs are usually applied with burnt umber. Dip the brush into a dab of the burnt umber and mix with a little medium on the palette. Pick up a little extra burnt umber on one side of the brush. Apply with a quick turning motion of the brush, leaving the extra burnt umber where the shadow should be deepest.

Veins are sometimes painted in with a fine brush using burnt umber or burnt sienna, or a mixture of both, or black. Other details may be painted in the same way.

V. *Adding details to gold leaf motifs with pen and India ink*

> *Materials:* Crow-quill pen
> Waterproof, varnishproof India ink, white or red ink

Apply the ink with fine crow-quill pen wherever fine line details are needed, over gold leaf which has had a coat of varnish, followed by a rubbing with pumice and water. Practice with the ink over a varnished surface before using, as inks differ greatly in flowing capacity.

VI. *Colored washes over gold leaf motifs*

Washes of the transparent colors may be used over varnished gold and aluminum leaf, as over bronze painting.

> *Materials:* #3 or #4 square-tipped showcard brush
> Medium (varnish and turpentine mixed)
> Transparent oil colors: Prussian blue, alizarin crimson, yellow lake
> For first method:
>   Varnish
>   Turpentine
> For second method:
>   Medium (half varnish, half turpentine)

Prussian blue with a little yellow lake makes a green wash over gold leaf. Verdigris over silver makes blue-green, but is not entirely transparent. Alizarin crimson, over silver, makes rosy red. Prussian blue is used over silver. Yellow lake is used over gold for yellow, and burnt umber is used over gold for brown. Add a little raw umber to dull these colors.

There are two ways of applying these transparent colors. If you want an all-over, even wash, use the following.

Dip a #3 square-tipped brush in turpentine and squeeze it out between the pages of an old phone book. Now dip it in varnish. (Don't wipe it on the edge of the can.) Brush it out on a slick magazine. Then apply the varnish in long strokes to the motif. Wipe out your brush between the pages of the magazine, so that its tip is flat and square. Dip *just the tip* in varnish and then in your mixed or plain transparent color. Brush it out on paper so that there is hardly any color in the brush. Now *dab* it onto the wet varnish motif lightly, so that just a little color shows. In a few minutes the dabs will blend into one color area.

The other method of applying transparent color leaves a darker area in some parts of the motif. Have some medium (half varnish and half turpentine) in a bottle cap. Dip your brush in this, then in color. Brush out a little on a magazine to make a thin wash. Pick up a little thicker color mixture at the tip of the brush and apply with a generous sweeping movement, following the contour of the fruit or flower being tinted, leaving the heavier color where shadows are indicated. Do not make any little separate strokes. Work quickly. Wipe off with a dry cloth at once if you wish to do it over.

In some early American work over gold, only part of a flower is so washed in color.

Delicate designs using gold leaf or bronzes

1. Leaves and flowers in brushed-on bronze

This little leaf design was found on an old tray used for candle-snuffers in a Winchester, Massachusetts, home. It is very like the design found on a bread tray in the Essex Institute at Salem. The latter is reproduced on page 136, but it is stenciled rather than painted. In this design, the large leaves are painted in black Serviceseal, or in a mixture of flat black paint with varnish. (The background of the original was also black.) When the tacky stage is reached, pale and rich gold are applied to the leaves. The lighter color is used on the upper part of the leaf, the darker below. Rub the bronze in sparingly with a piece of velvet, or chamois. The effect should be shadowy, darker where the veins of the leaves are. The small four-petal flowers and centers are also painted black, and powdered in silver solidly while tacky. The entire piece is varnished when dry.

When it dries, rub it down. Paint the small leaves near the silver flowers with a dark oxide of chromium green touched with a bit of raw umber and medium. The veins in the leaves and the curved lines surrounding

1. Leaves And Flowers in Brushed- On Bronze

2. Painted Design in Red, Gold, and Black on Gold Band

Delicate designs using gold leaf or bronzes, continued

the leaves are chrome yellow with a touch of raw umber added. *Apply with a very fine pointed brush. Finish as directed on pages 157–160.*

2. Painted design on gold band (from an old coaster now in the Museum of the Society for the Preservation of New England Antiquities, originally owned by Harrison Gray Otis).

A. Left half of design

The floral design between the left set of brackets is on a black background, the brackets being gold lines. Varnish the background and rub down as directed in Chapter 2. Paint the flower and leaves with pale gold bronze mixed with medium, using a #2 pointed quill brush. When almost dry, apply lemon-gold leaf by the method described in Chapter 3. Allow the gold leaf to set for several hours, then etch all the fine lines in the flower and leaves with a sharp-pointed tool. Varnish the area when the gold leaf has dried for 12 hours. Rub carefully with pumice. With a fine crow-quill pen and Crowell's Gold waterproof, varnishproof ink, or with a fine-pointed #1 brush, pale gold bronze and varnish, add the curlicues. If bronze is used, brush with dry bronze when nearly dry.

B. Right half of design

Apply background of gold between right set of brackets by painting with mixture of rich gold bronze and medium. When almost dry, lay rich gold leaf. (A good substitute method of obtaining the gold background would be to varnish first, then rub when almost dry with a piece of absorbent cotton saturated with rich gold bronze powder.) When the gold leaf has dried for at least 12 hours, varnish it and rub down with pumice carefully when dry. Paint the oval with black Serviceseal or with flat black mixed with varnish. Paint the two large leaves and the acorns the same. Allow to dry thoroughly. Paint the floral motif inside the black oval with pale gold bronze powder and medium. When almost dry apply lemon-gold leaf. (If you are not using gold leaf, apply extra bronze powder of the same color with a brush, while tacky.)

Using Venetian red with medium and a very fine #1 pointed quill brush, paint veins in the large black leaves, stem, and small leaves of the acorn, the crisscross pattern on the black acorn and the other small leaves. With a pen and waterproof black India ink or with a fine brush and drop- or ivory-black and medium, paint the curlicues. If the center flower is gold leaf, etch the lines into it with a sharp etching tool. If it is gold bronze paint, apply ink or paint as for the curlicues. Draw or paint in black one fine scalloped stripe an eighth of an inch inside each end of the gold background.

On the original coaster for a wine bottle, each half of the design is repeated twice. The design could, of course, be made smaller by reducing the size of the leaves or the spacing, or made larger by the addition of motifs. The red and black on gold, and the gold on black, make a very stunning finished article. For practical purposes, the whole design might be enlarged and used to trim a handsome living-room waste basket lined in gold, or it might be used as is on a desk set.

3. *Gold-leaf flower design with stenciled leaves (from a "sleigh" Empire toleware dish, Essex Institute, Salem; similar dish in Metropolitan Museum of Art, New York).*

The entire background is first painted black and then varnished. (See Chapter 1.) The center flower outlines are marked on according to transfer methods (Chapter 2), but the surrounding leaves are omitted. Paint the flower on the left and the one on the right in black Serviceseal or in flat black mixed with varnish. When it has reached the tacky stage, brush pale gold lining bronze onto the flower, with a chamois or velvet as in stenciling. Leave only a dark ring between the center group of petals and the lines radiating outward. Varnish the entire background and rub down with pumice and water. Tint the right-hand flower with alizarin crimson (a transparent oil color) and medium. Tint the left-hand flower with Prussian blue and medium. Refer to Chapter 8, pp. 127–128). When dry, varnish and rub down again.

Using a very fine #1 pointed quill brush and pale gold lining bronze with varnish (or crow-quill pen with waterproof and varnishproof gold ink, if preferred), draw in the fine lines for petals, the radiating lines on the outer petals and the outline of the flower, omitting the outline where the center flower overlaps the others. Varnish again and rub down.

Paint the center flower in rich gold bronze with medium, using a #3 pointed quill brush. When almost dry apply rich gold leaf to the entire

3. Gold Leaf Flowers, Stenciled Leaves, and Painted Acorns On A Distinguished Empire Toleware Dish

Delicate designs using gold leaf or bronzes, continued

flower, or brush on additional rich gold powder if you are not using gold leaf. If you have used gold leaf, etch the lines on the flower, when thorroughly dry, with a sharp-pointed tool before varnishing, draw in the lines with crow-quill pen and water and varnishproof ink, or paint the lines with #1 pointed brush, drop black, and medium. If you have used the rich gold powder, draw in the lines as above or paint with #1 pointed brush. If required, the outline of the petals, where they overlap, may be set off with an outline of black ink or black paint. Varnish the piece and rub it down.

Varnish it again and leave until tacky. Apply a small stenciled leaf with three points just outside the flowers, leaving the center of each leaf dark for veins, but brushing the tips brightly with rich gold bronze. Fill in as much space as desired with such leaves. Be sure that a little of the background appears between the leaves so that one may be distinguished from another. Apply the veins to these leaves by brushing gold around a bit of curved linen wherever you wish to place a vein. Stencil the small flowers at the top in silver bronze.

While the background is still tacky, apply gold bronze out beyond the end of the stenciled leaves to fill in the remaining space, all except a narrow quarter-inch edge, which should be wiped clean of bronze and striped. Brush a little antique copper bronze into the space (which has been left unfilled) above and below the center flower. Let dry 12 hours, then varnish. Rub down.

Finally, paint the very small design entirely with black oil color and medium, using a #1 pointed quill brush, omitting only the crisscross lines on the acorn and the veins in the leaves. Paint the short lines and brush strokes around flowers also. When the black dries, paint these omitted details in English vermilion oil color and medium or draw with crow-quill pen and vermilion water- and varnishproof ink.

The small design on the circular ends of the dish is to be painted in pale gold bronze mixed with medium.

A fine gold stripe on the edge completes the pattern.

Finish with varnish coats rubbed down according to directions.

Chinese design for oblong tray with round corners
with gold leaf, painting, and stenciling

Paint background black, very dark green or Chinese red. (See directions for base coats and varnishing, pp. 16–19.)

Enlarge design four times present size.

Trace the four roses, the woman's fan, the tree in the center, and all scattered groups of leaves onto the tray. Paint them in with rich gold bronze powder mixed with medium (half turpentine, half varnish). When dried to tacky state, brush dry gold onto these motifs with a soft camel's hair brush.

When this has dried completely, brush away the excess powder with a very soft cloth or brush, and wash gently with mild soap and lukewarm water.

Paint the faces of the people putty color, using titanium white, with a touch of raw sienna and raw umber added, mixing with medium.

After 24 hours, varnish the tray. Rub it down, following directions on page 159.

Cut, out of architect's linen, several different wavy-edged stencils from which to make the clouds, hills, and waves, more or less as follows:

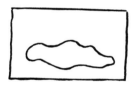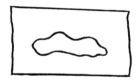

Varnish the tray and wait until it has reached the tacky stage. Apply the stencils one at a time, always placing first the one which appears to be forward of the others. Using very little bronze pale gold lining, or Venus 57, polish in over the cut edges of the stencil lightly, blending into the black as soon as you have defined the edge of the wavy line. Apply the bronze only where you want the edges to show—either top or bottom, or both as in the case of the small clouds. After you have stenciled the foremost hill, or cloud, or wave, lay the next stencil just above and "in back" of it. You may use your imagination a good deal in doing this, but practice first on a piece of black tin or painted black paper or cardboard. (Read directions for stenciling before starting.) Be sure to place the stencils in the same relative positions as in the pattern, so that the buildings, people, trees, and flowers will be well placed.

Allow the tray to dry about 48 hours. Do not *rub down with pumice over the design, or you may scratch it. Wash the tray with mild soap and warm water, being careful of the stenciling. If there is unwanted gold on the background which will not wash off, paint out such mistakes with the same flat paint used for the background.*

Varnish the tray again. Dry thoroughly. Rub it down.

Trace the outlines of the building, summer house and steps, human figures, the boat with man, the large leaves below the roses, and the centers of the roses. Paint these with a #2 or #3 quill brush in pale gold lining bronze, applied with the medium. (You will be applying gold leaf to these, so only do one or two at a time, lest they dry before you are ready to do them all.) When a motif dries to the tacky stage, lay lemon-gold leaf over it, according to directions for applying leaf (pp. 82–83). Follow directions also for removing excess leaf. After 48 hours, varnish the tray. When thoroughly dry—24 to 48 hours—rub it down with pumice and water. Cover up any mistakes with the background paint.

Using a fine crow-quill pen, draw in all the little black lines, freehand, with varnishproof, waterproof black India ink on the gold leaf and on the painted roses. Dry.

With waterproof, varnishproof gold ink and crow-quill pen, draw in the five other trees, the tiny groups of flowers that look like pincushions, and the short straight lines representing water. Also add any little lines needed to embellish the groups of leaves.

Finally, using a ruling pen and raised ruler (except for rounded corners), surround the entire pattern with three or four very fine stripes in the gold ink. (Striping on these old trays often cut across a little of the pattern.) Paint a narrow gold stripe around the outside edge of the tray. (See striping directions, pp. 38–39.) Use pale gold lining bronze, either with the medium or with plain varnish. When tacky, either brush with the same dry bronze, or apply gold leaf to the stripe.

Allow to dry 48 hours. Then varnish the entire tray with four to six coats, treating each coat as directed under finishing processes.

94

CHAPTER

Stenciling in bronze

I. Tracing a stencil onto architect's linen

Materials: Tracing paper
White paper
Architect's linen
Pen and ink, or hard pencil

Trace each separate part of a design for stenciling onto tracing paper, with a sharp pencil or with a croquille pen and India ink. If you have a complete pattern traced from a piece of furniture or from a tray, or a photograph of one, it must first be broken down into its separate units before tracing. If part of a fruit or flower is hidden behind another part of the design, supply the missing part of it in making a copy.

Lay a piece of architect's linen, with margin at least an inch larger than the unit to be traced, over each unit of the design separately. Trace each one, preferably in India ink, delineating each line clearly. If you place a sheet of white paper underneath all, the design will show up well.

II. *Making an impression of a stencil already cut*

Avoid tracing inside the cutout design, as it stretches the linen. A quick method is to press a small cellulose sponge on an ink-pad and then through the stencil onto your own piece of linen. Clean the stencil at once.

Another simple method is to take a piece of absorbent cotton or velvet, dip it in dark-color bronze powder and rub through the stencil onto your dry linen, being very careful to rub inward from the edges of the design so that pointed edges will remain flat. Use the powder sparingly, or it will leak under the stencil and blur the image. Clean it from the stencil with turpentine, carbona, or painter's thinner. The design will be visible on the linen, but if the powder does not make the design clear enough, outline it while fresh with pencil or pen.

Stencils may also be traced by placing the linen directly over the stencil, with the shiny side down. Use India ink for tracing as it marks the linen more clearly.

III. *Cutting a stencil*

> *Materials:* Sharp, pointed embroidery or manicure scissors, razor blade in a holder, or Exacto knife #11 or #16
> Sharpening stone or fine sandpaper, for sharpening scissors

Try all of these tools for cutting stencils, as you may find one much easier to use than another. Some like very sharp, small embroidery scissors with straight points. I prefer fine curved manicure scissors with short blade and longer handle. Others will cut only with an Exacto knife or razor blade fastened in a holder. Exacto or razor blades must be sharpened on a stone frequently, or discarded, as they dull quickly and cause the linen to pucker. Scissors may be sharpened by cutting fine sandpaper.

In using a knife or razor blade, the tracing on architect's linen is place on a slick-paper magazine. Hold the linen down firmly and draw the blade toward you, turning the tracing as you go around curves, rather than turning the cutting arm. When the knifepoint reaches a corner, stop and turn the tracing around so that the knife will continue to be drawn toward you. On very fine lines, you may use the knife for one side of the cut, then cut the other side of the line with fine scissors, if you find it easier than making both sides of the cut with the knife.

In cutting out a stencil with scissors, follow the same rule of turning the piece of linen, rather than turning the hand that holds the scissors. Even very tiny circles may be cut with curving scissors if you turn the work around. When you start to cut out any small motif, first make an incision in the middle of it with the point of the scissors, then cut to the edge. In this way you are not so likely to mar the stencil as if you made the first cut directly on the traced line.

There are several ways of making tiny round holes, such as the dots in the centers of flowers. They may be punched through from the right side (the dull side) of the linen with a large needle, then sanded smooth on the back with fine #00 sandpaper, or trimmed on the back with blades of small scissors. A hand punch struck lightly with a hammer over a piece of lead will also take small circles out neatly. Or you may use a leatherworker's punch, some of which are adjustable to different-size holes.

IV. Applying the stencil

Materials: Varnish: Supervalspar, or preferably, a "soft" varnish
1" or 1½" good varnish brush
Piece of firm silk millinery velvet, hemmed, or a soft piece of chamois skin
Stencils, cut out as above

Turpentine, Carbona for removing slips

Bronze powders: must be powders of fine, silky grind, rather than the kind sold for painting molded figurines. (Higher code numbers on the jar usually indicate finer powders; fine powder also clings to the sides of the jar when shaken. Judge the color of the powder by applying a touch of it to a dark surface, or by its appearance from the outside of the jar; or rub a little on your finger. Lining bronze indicates fine grind.)

1. Pale gold lining bronze, such as Venus #57 (this color is sometimes called "lemon gold")
2. Brushed brass, or "rich" gold
3. Chromium (a nontarnishing bright silver), or aluminum (which tarnishes)

Three of the bronze powders listed will start you off on your stenciling. When you become more ambitious and choose more difficult projects, you may also need:

"Brilliant fire" and copper, or antique copper bronzes, and possibly some of the real colors. The latter are hard to apply without having a garish look, but are improved by mixing with gold or silver.

The metallic bronzes are combined for gradual shading from one to another. Silver is often mixed with gold for burnished fruit. Brilliant fire, mixed with copper or antique copper, gives a softly glowing copper color.

Stenciling, since it uses varnish as a base, requires a warm, dry, and dust-free environment. The can of varnish should be set in a coffee can of hot water for a few minutes before using. Do not shake the varnish.

Place a small amount of your different colors of bronze down the center fold of a piece of drapery velour. This may be kept, folded, in your equipment box when not in use. If velour is un-available, put a little of each color out on a paper towel to use.

Varnish the surface to be stenciled, using a fine varnish brush and Supervalspar, unless a soft varnish such as Clear Serviceseal is available. Varnish very smoothly, in the same careful manner in which you put on the preparation coat over the flat enamel. Blow on the surface to smooth the varnish, and put the article in a warm, clean place.

The stenciling is done with the velvet or chamois skin wrapped around the index finger. When the varnish is ready for the stencil, your finger will barely cling to it when lightly applied. Or press a bit of architect's linen to it—it should cling a little, but leave no mark when removed. Work quickly when this stage is reached, for it soon passes.

1. *A one-piece stencil*

For your first attempt, choose a one-piece stencil, and fill in all the spaces solidly. Press the stencil shiny side down onto the varnish, smoothing the cut edges so it will adhere. Dip your velvet-wrapped finger lightly into the bronze and rub it on a newspaper or on the back of your hand to remove loose grains of powder. It is very easy to use too much bronze. With a polish-ing motion, smooth on the bronze, starting on the linen and work-ing out into the open area. Never reverse the direction, or bronze powder will work under your stencil, and the cut edges will become ruffled. When all the open areas are uniformly bronzed, raise a corner of the linen with your fingernail and carefully re-move the stencil. Remove any errors according to instructions (p. 120). Clean off the stencil with cotton moistened with Carbona or turpentine.

You have now completed a simple stencil. Wash with soap when dry. It may be tinted with transparent oil colors if desired (see p. 121). Varnish (p. 120).

An Easy One-Piece Stencil

An easy one-piece stencil

This simple design was stenciled on an old tin document box, shaped like an old-fashioned trunk with an arched lid. The stencil is cut in one piece. It is stenciled in two colors of bronze, and has added painted details. The background is asphaltum. This design is very easy to complete, excellent for a beginner.

1. Cutting the stencil. Cut the entire pattern, except the smallest dot in the center of the flower and the half-circle of tiny dots.

2. Stenciling. Stencil over varnish which has been allowed to dry to the tacky stage. (See Chapter 8.) Stencil centers of flowers in rich gold bronze. Polish the petals outward from the sawtooth edge with rich gold, shading into deep gold (which has an orange hue). Polish everything in this stencil solidly. Stencil the leaves in rich gold. (When dry, varnish the stencil and rub down according to directions.)

3. Painted details. Combine Prussian blue with Indian yellow or gamboge. Apply this green with a fat #3 pointed quill brush in a sweeping circular motion to the center area of the flowers, just overlapping the sawtooth part of the petals. When dry, paint dots in chrome yellow with a pointed #1 quill brush. Apply center dot the same. Stripe around with a very fine stripe of country yellow or transparent chrome yellow, with a striping brush.

4. Trim. Sides of box were bordered with fine yellow stripes. Pointed brush strokes radiated from the top handle outward.

Courtesy of Society for Preservation of New England Antiquities, Boston, Mass.

New England apple basket

The original apple basket was stenciled on a transparent deep blue background, but the background may be black, red, or dark green.

For the transparent blue coat, add a small amount of good Prussian blue oil color to a little varnish. Mix well, then add this to more varnish. Brush on very smoothly, blowing, on each section as varnished, to blend the strokes together. (Transparent varnish must be put on over very bright, new tin.) Dry, and rub down. Varnish and rub again (p. 18).

The stencil for the sides is cut in one piece, the single stripe ¼ inch from the edge being painted. Apply the stencil in place, following directions on page 99. Polish the entire design in solidly, rubbing from the solid linen toward the cut edges. For the two large center flowers, use pale gold lining bronze. Then mix a little antique copper and brilliant fire bronze with rich gold, to make a color as near pale orange as possible. Stencil the two outside flowers with this. The remaining leaves and stems are done in rich gold. Stencil the trim just below the design in pale gold lining bronze. Stencil the pattern on bottom in pale gold lining. Remove errors.

After 24 hours or more in a warm, dry place, wash off excess gold with warm water and soap. Dry. Varnish and rub down.

With #3 square-tipped quill brush, paint the left center flower carefully with varnish, having first dipped the brush in turpentine and wiped it nearly dry, then having dipped it in varnish and brushed it out on a slick-finish magazine. Apply in long strokes. Now wipe your brush out between the pages of a magazine so that it is flat and square. Dip just the tip in varnish and then in a mixture of alizarin crimson and a tiny bit of burnt umber and yellow lake. When mixed with varnish and painted over pale gold, this should be a rusty rose color. Wipe brush on magazine so that there is hardly any color left. Dab this onto the wet, varnished flower very lightly so that just a little color shows, leaving all the tips of the petals gold. In a few minutes the dabs will blend into each other. Use Prussian blue with a speck of raw umber on right center flower in same way.

Paint one inner stripe in English vermilion, edging stripe in pale gold, with #0 striping brush.

Allow to dry thoroughly. Varnish and finish (pp. 157–162).

New England Apple Basket—
design for four sides and bottom

PAINTED
DETAILS

=W

ONLY
EXTRA
STENCIL

A STENCIL CUT IN ONE PIECE

A stencil cut in one piece and rosette border

This large stencil was found on a tin tray in the museum of the Society for the Preservation of New England Antiquities. It is rather elementary in nature and not an example of perfect design, but would be good practice for a beginner in cutting out and applying a stencil, as it requires no shading or placement of units in the process of stenciling.

A few details are painted: the round red flower, the white transparent brush strokes on the fruit, the small groups of three berries (labeled W), the curlicues, and dots. The gold leaves have one long pointed brush stroke of dark green through them, following the broken outline.

Directions

Paint background black. Follow processes on pages 16–18. Cut the entire stencil, except flowers, curlicues, and painted berries. Cut one small scalloped medallion for repeat border.

Apply stenciled design solidly in rich gold bronze powder. Remove errors. When stencil is thoroughly dry, give the article a coat of varnish. Dry 24 hours. Rub down. Trace flowers, berries, and tendrils in place. Paint flowers red, using cadmium red light oil color mixed with medium. Using oxide of chromium green with a little raw umber, paint five large brush strokes of green through the center of the five long-leaf sprays as dotted lines indicate. (A transparent mixture of Prussian blue and gamboge (yellow) would probably make a more artistic tint over these leaves, but the original is as described.) When red flowers are completely dry, paint brush strokes and dots transparent white. Paint small groups of three berries, marked W, in transparent white also.

When paint is thoroughly dry, paint the tendrils with a mixture of pale gold lining bronze and medium. When almost dry, brush extra dry gold over the tendrils. (These tendrils in the original were dotted lines.)

Varnish the entire piece. Dry. Rub down. Varnish again and allow to dry until tacky. Apply the small medallions to the border, after measuring to see how near together they may be placed to come out evenly on the border. Use pale gold lining bronze for border.

2. *A composite stencil*

For your first venture with a composite stencil, choose simple shapes, such as peaches, melons, cherries, apples, and leaves. (The traditional fruits of early American stenciling are listed by Janet Waring in her book—the strawberry, cherry, bilberry, apple, plum, pear, and lemon.)

Choose a basket or urn stencil to hold the fruit. Place this in the lower center of the object you are stenciling, after your varnish has reached the perfect, tacky stage. Smooth it on, so it will adhere everywhere, and so that no powder can get underneath it.

Wrap your piece of velvet around your finger, touch it to the bronze, and wipe it against a newspaper as before. With a polishing motion, smooth the basket or urn design in quite solidly, again starting on the linen and working outward into the open spaces. Clean and remove the stencil as before.

Stencil the foremost fruit next—the foremost object always comes first in a grouping of fruit or flowers. Place the stencil and polish in its highlights first, burnishing the lightest parts with the velvet. Burnish the edges very lightly to give the fruit shape. Where there are shadows, leave the area almost dark, but gently powder them so that they are not completely dark. (It is helpful to study pictures of fruit, and also the effects of light on real fruit.)

Fill in the bowl with other fruits, placing smaller fruits outward in the bowl. Where one fruit comes near another, the part which is in shadow must taper off into near-darkness.

Arrange several varieties of leaf around the outside of the fruit arrangement, without using too much bronze powder. Burnish the tips and edges of the leaves brightly. The base of the leaf is usually without a definite outline, and the center of the leaf is left darkest, so that veins will show up better when applied. Leaves may be reversed to give variation, after cleaning them.

The veins are polished in around the outside of a smooth curved piece of architect's linen. They are sometimes painted in, in "old yellow."

After the leaves, if some filling on the edges is needed, select small sprays of wheat or tiny flowers to go around the arrangement. Squint at the whole from time to time to see where balance is needed.

Next, try an oval arrangement of fruit and flowers, completely surrounded by leaves. Border patterns may also be made, by repeating groups of fruit at regular intervals.

Stenciling a bunch of grapes, with their leaves, provides excellent practice in light and shadow. First decide where the largest and foremost grapes will be, after studying pictures or well-stenciled pieces. Cut different-size circles for the grapes. Stencil from the center of the bunch down to the tip, then proceed up to the top of the bunch, and out from the center. Burnish the edges of those which are foremost. The grapes farthest back will show only in part. Use two or three different leaf shapes, the tips of the outer ones barely showing. Stems, veins, and tendrils may be stenciled, or painted in using "old yellow." Sometimes a tiny yellow or white painted highlight is added on grapes and cherries.

Some fruits are cut in two or more separate parts. In cutting an apricot or peach, an oval may be cut for the foremost, highlighted part. The smaller part showing is a crescent shape, which is only faintly bronzed. (The oval *may* be used for both halves of the fruit, however bronzing in only part of the oval for the part of the fruit away from the light. Touch the edges somewhat with bronze.)

Interest is given to the stenciling by the use of different colors of bronze. In a fruit pattern, those fruits which are at the center

of interest might be silver, while others could be done in brushed brass or pale gold, which is actually a good medium shade of gold. Leaves may be shaded from gold to orange gold, blending bronze powders as you change from one color to another. In general, avoid making abrupt changes in color, as from silver to bright orange gold, or from gold to red, without blending gradually. Brilliant fire bronze is used for small accents, and when blended with gold is used for the highlights on some of the brighter fruits.

Stems and leaves of fruit, centers of flowers, and other details are sometimes cut out separately from the fruit and applied in a different bronze color. Details are stenciled *first* when it is necessary to make them stand out, as when over highlighted parts of a fruit. For example, a solid piece of architect's linen in the shape of a strawberry is cut out, and tiny holes are pierced in it for seeds. Stencil through these holes firmly with rich gold. Remove this detail stencil. Next, apply a detail stencil of stem and leaves at top in gold. Place the actual strawberry stencil over the area and apply brilliant fire bronze over all, allowing the gold "seeds" and the tiny leaves at the top to shine through.

Naturally, details will show up well, whenever applied, if they are over a shadowed area.

Pattern from a stenciled Hitchcock chair

Urn of Fruit and Flowers

1. Cutting the stencil. *Cut all the separate units shown on page 111, plus fruit from the other bowl design as needed. If you desire to use the leaf border at the ends of main slat, cut three or four serrated peaks—with ovals cut from them—from the edge of a 1½-inch strip of architect's linen. For the top rail, cut everything but the two concentric ellipses (page 112, center). Cut the pattern for the seat rail.*

2. Background. *Paint the chair black, or black over red, as described in Chapter 2. Leave the main slat black.*

(*continued*)

3. Stenciling. Varnish the back slat for the principal design. Stencil the bowl solidly in pale gold lining bronze, all except the dash-dot motif just below the main rim, which is cut separately. Stencil it in chromium bronze, solidly. Stencil the melon, shading as indicated and allowing it to fade out where the leaf is to go, in pale gold with a little chromium mixed in. Stencil peach with same, leaving shadows dim as shown. Stencil top half of pear in pale gold, shading to darkness, leaving room for leaf. Stencil leaf in rich gold shading into darkness where ribs should be. Add quince in pale gold, leaving dark space for blossom-end details. Stencil the latter solidly. Add grapes, beginning with the one nearest center, placing each one carefully so that they look natural. Highlight each one. Grapes may be chromium if desired or chromium and silver mixture. Add large flowers and cherries, then large outer leaves beneath flowers, followed by leaf veins. Flowers may be silver if desired (chromium bronze), and leaves a mixture of pale and rich gold. Fill in with sprays of small flowers and leaves as the composition requires. Frame the fruit in the bowl with leaves, which are mostly shadowed, except for the tips. Polish the latter brightly.

4. Trim. (See designs on p. 112.) Varnish the top and seat rails and allow to dry until tacky. Stencil the design on the top rail and seat rail solidly in rich gold bronze. Allow to dry 24 hours or more if necessary. Varnish over these areas again. Varnish the main slat also. Allow to dry thoroughly as above, then rub down with pumice and damp cotton.

Paint the brush stroke trim on the side posts, using #3 quill brush dipped in medium, then in rich gold bronze. Paint the straight band with #4 square-tipped brush, below this, leaving 2 inches of the smooth part of side posts blank, above and below this band. Paint the turnings on the seat rail and on the front legs with the same gold, and the turnings at the bottom of the side posts. When the gold is nearly dry, brush it with some dry gold bronze on a soft brush. After 24 hours, wash the gold gently with mild soap and warm water to remove excess gold. Varnish side posts.

Using #1 quill brush with old yellow and medium, paint the two ellipses on the top rail stencil. Paint a fine stripe as a border around this design and around the side post trim, following the contour of the chair. Add narrow stripes of yellow on either side of all gold turnings. Paint a little square on the blocks at the seat corners. Paint narrow stripe border around main stencil. Dry. Varnish entire chair with dull varnish.

Stencil Motifs for Urn of Fruit and Flowers

DESIGN FOR ROLL OF CHAIR SEAT

DESIGN FOR TOP RAIL

TRIM FOR CHAIR WITH URN OF FRUIT AND FLOWERS

PAINTED TRIM
FOR SIDE POSTS

7" LONG

3. *Border patterns*

Border patterns which are continuous, without change in the size of motif, are the easiest to handle. Decide how far from the edge you wish to place such a border and continually measure with a small piece of architect's linen cut as a gauge to be sure you are applying it evenly. Such stencils are usually cut in three- or four-inch lengths and must be guided around curved edges by continually turning the stenciled object in order to bring the straight stencil into phase with the contours of the object.

Turning corners requires a good deal of practice. If possible, try to arrange the pattern so that the middle of a small motif does not come right at the turn of the corner, but is completed first. If it is necessary to eliminate a small portion of a motif in order to turn the corner without placing one motif directly over another, do so by placing a bit of clean architect's linen under the part of the motif which you are eliminating, so that it will leave no mark.

If the border design consists of small motifs plus a larger motif at intervals, it will be necessary to plan where the larger ones fall. Measure the distance along the sides and ends, and plan to place the motifs at the side centers and end centers, or at regular intervals. The resulting extra space may be filled by repeating some of the smaller pattern or by using appropriate additional motifs. If the pattern should be overcrowded, some of it may be deleted. Try the stencil out on paper, cut to the size of the object, if you are doubtful of the fit of your stencils.

4. *Stencils requiring unusual treatment*

Some early American stencil designs, especially in border patterns, are cut in outline form and may be stenciled within and surrounded by a bronze cloud of the same color. Butterflies and other fragile forms are particularly adaptable to this technique.

Stencil Motifs for Urn of Fruit and Leaves

In such cases, no margin may be left outside the pattern. Cut the fine inner details of the pattern, then the narrow outside edge, since it would be crumpled if held while cutting the inside details.

If you wish to stencil a butterfly design or some other small motif on a solid gold band, varnish a broad band for a border—a little wider than your motif. Cut out pieces of architect's linen in the shape of the butterfly stencil, but solid and a little larger. When varnish is tacky, put these solid stencils in place and rub gold bronze over the rest of the varnish band, with chamois, velvet, or sable brush. Remove the linen butterfly "masks" and apply the actual cutout stencil to the dark areas left. The edges of the dark areas may be softened by applying a little gold bronze to them with a piece of velvet.

An alternative method for applying small stencil motifs to dark areas on top of gold is to paint the shape of the small motif solidly with black varnish or Serviceseal on top of a completed gold band after the latter has dried. When the black area becomes tacky, use the small stencil on it.

Sometimes a flower or bird is stenciled in one color, its details stenciled in a contrasting bronze, and a cloud of still a different bronze surrounds the whole. Cut out a *solid shape* exactly the same as the flower or bird stencil, piercing it with the details,

Pattern from an old stenciled chair belonging to the author
Urn of fruit with leaves

1. Cutting the stencil. *Cut all the parts shown on the illustration of separate units. The original chair has no additional trim on the main slat, except a fine yellow stripe. Top and seat rails are decorated with the same stenciled pattern with painted ellipses that decorates the top rail of the chair with urn of fruit and flowers (see p. 112). This little pattern resembling brush strokes is frequently found on the top and seat rail of Hitchcocks. The side posts are also trimmed with simple yellow stripes ending in a* V *at the lower end. A solid bar of gold (illustrated) is painted inside the yellow stripes.*

Do not cut the diamond pattern in one with the urn. (continued)

2. Stenciling. *Varnish the central slat and allow to dry until tacky. Stencil all but the diamond shapes of the bowl in rich gold, shading the lower part slightly as shown. Polish the top rim and foot solidly with gold. Next, apply the diamond stencil to the bowl, starting at the bottom with pale gold and working from it up to chromium at the top. Stencil the pear next, using a mixture of rich gold and pale gold bronze, highlighting as noted in the sketch. Stencil the peach in two parts and the melon in pale gold. Next, stencil the central "apple" in pale gold, leaving it dark in the center, but highlighted at the top center with a little brilliant fire bronze. Apply center detail very clearly in pale gold. Stencil the apple on right side of bowl last, all in pale gold.*

Apply leaves so that they fill the space nicely. Do not make them too bright. Polish the tips the most, in rich gold bronze. A second row of leaf tips may extend behind the first. Add the veins as shown, wherever there is enough leaf to justify using them. Tendrils, solidly bronzed, fill in the remaining open spaces.

3. Trim. *(See p. 118.) Stencil top and seat rail designs. Dry.*

Paint the brush stroke design and the gold bar on the side posts with #3 quill brush, using pale gold lining bronze and medium. Paint the turnings on the front chair legs and on the seat rail in the same gold, using a larger brush. When all these are nearly dry, brush some dry gold over them with a soft brush. After at least 24 hours, wash off the extra gold, gently, with warm water and mild soap. Dry thoroughly and varnish the side posts and the chair turnings, as well as the stenciled areas. Rub down with pumice and damp cotton, when thoroughly dry.

Now, using old yellow and a very narrow striping brush or scroller, paint the two elliptical lines around the top and seat rail stencils. Paint a very fine stripe around the principal design also, about $1/4$ inch from the top and bottom of the slat and $3/4$ inch in from the ends. Paint a narrow outline stripe around the top rail also. Outline the side posts with a narrow stripe near the edge which ends in a point just above the turnings on the posts. Paint narrow stripes of yellow on both sides of all gilded turnings, and on the corner blocks of the seat.

Allow to dry at least 24 hours, more if necessary. Varnish the entire chair with dull varnish. (If you desire to antique the chair, use Supervalspar for the first coat, with a little burnt umber oil color added to it.) Allow to dry as above. Rub this coat down with pumice and damp cotton. Use dull varnish for the finish coat.

116

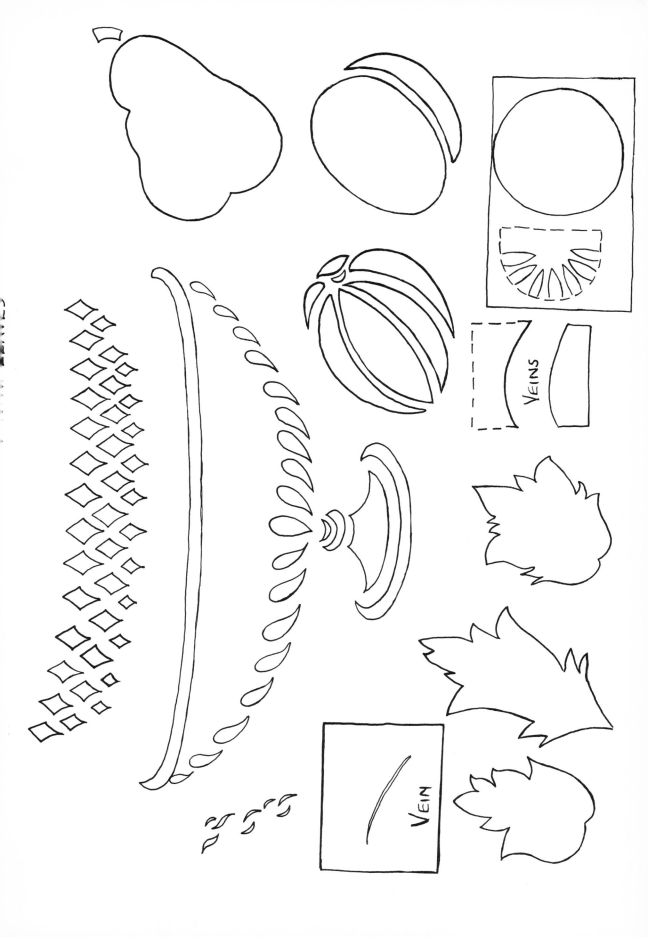

VEINS

VEIN

Top Rail Stencil

Seat Rail Stencil

Same as Above After Painting Stripes

Trims
for
Chair
Stenciled with
Urn of Fruit
with Leaves

Painted Decoration for Side Posts

such as petals and stamens for a flower, or wing, tailfeathers and eye for a bird. Apply this *first* and rub chromium bronze through the pierced parts. Next, stencil the flower or bird itself in gold. Finally, replace the solid shape of the flower or bird and gently apply a cloud of chromium bronze around the outside, polishing a little near the edge, but fading out to nothing. In the late period of stenciling, brilliant fire bronze was used for cloud effects, but it often looks gaudy. This method is called *reverse stenciling*.

5. *Stenciled scenic views*

Some stencils take the form of bucolic scenes, such as a girl swinging in a cottage garden, a couple in a horse-drawn carriage with a full moon overhead, a pretty miss in a garden with hollyhocks nodding over a picket fence, a pair of children having tea with a kitten by their side, or a landscape of cottage, hill, and clouds. These greatly resemble the primitive paintings of our American ancestors. Though they have no great artistic merit, they seem to be very popular today, as they were in the nineteenth century. These complicated scenes were frequently found on rectangular "sandwich trays," with rounded corners and keyhole openings at the ends. The different parts of such stencils are, of course, cut and applied separately. They may be adapted for a variety of spaces by deleting units of the pattern, or by adding more clouds, flowers, trees, and so on.

6. *Stencils cut in one piece*

You may come across some stencils whose many parts are cut all in one piece. These were much used at the time Hitchcock chairs and Boston rockers were turned out in factories in quantities because of the speed with which they could be applied by inexperienced women. I suggest that you spurn the use of most of these patterns, but take from them any parts which are well shaped and combine them with other stencil motifs. Many such patterns are of poor design, and include meaningless touches. In general they represent the factory approach to decoration.

V. *Removing and correcting errors made in stenciling*

> *Materials:* Soap and water
> Turpentine
> Paint of exact background color
> Cotton-wrapped toothpicks

A good washing with mild soap will frequently remove traces of extra bronze powder from the background entirely. Very slight errors, or loose bits of bronze, may be removed immediately after picking up the stencil by carefully using a cotton-wrapped toothpick which has been dipped in turpentine. Great care must be taken not to remove some of the design by mistake, before it dries. Never use Carbona except away from the design, as it will prevent varnish from drying. When the varnish is dry, Carbona can be *quickly* and *lightly* used if further corrections are needed.

A stenciling job is seldom so perfect that no cover-up work is required, but reduce the work to a minimum by using care. To cover mistakes, use the exact color of the background. Fill in places where bronze is not meant to be, using a tiny brush for small places. If extra bronze is in a good many places on the plain area, cover the entire background around the design with another coat, in order to avoid a splotchy look to your piece. Avoid leaving raised areas on the background.

VI. *Varnishing over the stencil*

After the stencil is completely dry, when errors have been re-moved or painted over and the article is thoroughly dry again, a coat of varnish is given the stencil. Follow the exact directions for varnishing given in Chapter 2, *Varnishing over flat coats* (pp. 18–19). After varnish dries, rub very gently with finest wet and dry sandpaper which has been wet and then rubbed on a wet cake of Ivory soap. Rub until the tray feels smooth all over, and the top gloss has disappeared. Be careful not to rub through the varnish.

VII. *Tinting of stencils*

Materials: #3 or #5 square-tipped quill or tray painter brush

Transparent artist's oil colors given below

For first method: medium (half varnish, half turpentine)

For second method: varnish, turpentine.

Transparent oil colors are always used in tinting stencils. There are many different colors available in bronze powders, but except for silver and various shades of gold and copper, including brilliant fire, colors on the old pieces were usually obtained, more softly, by the use of transparent oils *over* silver and gold as follows:

Green (usually over gold)	Prussian blue plus yellow lake
Blue-green (over silver)	Verdigris
Red	Alizarin crimson
Blue	Prussian blue
Yellow	Yellow lake
Brown	Burnt umber

Any of these colors may be dulled by adding raw umber.

Transparent washes are usually applied over stencils which have been very completely polished with bronze powder. A shadowed effect may be obtained by the use of more color on the *tip* of the brush. An even effect is had by using a drier brush.

Pattern from a very fine stenciled side chair

This chair (Harrison Gray Otis House, Boston, Mass., courtesy Society for the Preservation of New England Antiquities) is one of the finest examples of stenciling that I have seen, shading as it does from one color of gold to another with great delicacy and filling the space of the main slat with such variety and interest.

The decorative trim for the top rail and for the front of the chair seat is laid in gold leaf over a mixture of pale gold bronze painted on with medium and left until almost dry. The trim for the side posts, (1) on the illustration of chair trims (p. 135), is delicate: a band of gold painted with fine black veins and striped with a fine black line. The brush strokes beneath it are applied in gold leaf. The background is black with slight streaks of red, except for the main slat, which is black.

1. Cutting the stencil units. *The following list of units may help you. (See Chapter 4.)*

> *Units: The pear and stem, large apple, top detail for apple, apple on left (turned around for left half), the details for the two-part apple, three sizes of grape, two straight stems, the curving grape tendril, group of three strawberries, groups of stems, petals, seeds and leaves to match, the starlike flower, separate center details for it, four-petaled flower, large single sweeping leaf plus a curved piece of linen for its vein, other leaf, group of veins to fit leaf. See the details for veins for the urn of fruit with leaves (p. 117).*

2. Stenciling. *Varnish the back slat, which is plain black, and allow to dry until tacky. (With so complicated a stencil, it will be necessary to work fast before the varnish dries, so practice once on cardboard or tin before final stenciling.) Lay the pear in place. Polish all highlights solidly with pale gold, fading out toward shadows and toward large leaf and apple. Polish stem with rich gold. Apply blossom details to pear solidly, with rich gold. Lay the large apple in place and polish lower center highlight with pale gold, also a narrow area just above the blossom details. Allow the bronze to fade out toward shadows, touching with gold just at the rim. Leave blossoms shadowy. Apply the details in rich gold, without any shading. Lay right half of other apple, and polish from highlights to shadow with pale gold bronze. Using round side of apple leftward, apply gold more faintly for left half of apple. Apply blossom detail solidly in rich gold. Place center grapes below each apple, highlighting with pale gold. Add stems in solid pale*

(continued)

FINE STENCILED CHAIR WITH VARIETY OF FRUIT

Design for Back of Fine Stenciled Chair

gold, then other grapes along stem. *Lay group of strawberries at each end (reversing stencil after cleaning with Carbona, for opposite side) polishing brightly with rich gold at tips, fading to shadow at 'stem end. Lay group of details for strawberries, including large strawberry leaves, exactly in place. Polish solidly in pale gold, except leaves, which are shaded in centers. Lay star-shaped flowers, polishing at tips with pale gold. Then lay their details and polish in with rich gold solidly. Tuck in the four-lobed flowers here and there where needed, polishing* least *in part of petals nearest center, using rich gold. Surround the entire pattern with leaves, largely in shadow, applied in pale gold. Apply veins in pale gold. Apply curving tendrils near bunches of grapes, polishing with rich gold. Take care that one fruit does not show through another. Lay each unit carefully with thought for the piece that will be laid next to it. Fruit details should be stenciled before fruit. Place carefully.*

Varnish the corner blocks of the chair seat. When tacky, polish the edges of the large leaf in pale gold bronze. Apply the veins brightly in the same gold, turning the single vein stencil different ways to make all the veins.

Varnish over entire design when thoroughly dry. Rub down.

3. Painted details. *If necessary, the large center leaf may be outlined very finely in black with a #1 quill brush, where it adjoins the fruit. Paint a quarter-inch gold stripe around the entire edge of the slat after this line dries, using #3 striper, pale gold bronze, and medium. When stripe is nearly dry, apply gold leaf to it, or brush with dry gold bronze if preferred. Paint the gold motifs onto the side posts, top rail, and front of chair seat, with #3 quill brush. Smaller brush for fine details. (Motif for side post is (1) on page 135.) When nearly dry, apply gold leaf, or treat as above. Stripe the turnings on the legs, front rung, top rail, and side posts with gold bronze and medium, using #4 quill brush. Brush with dry bronze when nearly dry.*

After 24 hours or more, wash off excess dry bronze with warm water and mild soap. Varnish over all painted areas. Rub down.

Paint the fine lines on side post decoration in black with #1 brush. Paint a fine stripe in old yellow with a very narrow striping brush around the side posts, corner blocks, sides of chair seats, main slat, and on both sides of all gold turnings. When dry, varnish the entire chair with dull varnish. (If you wish to antique the decoration, use a little burnt umber in a first coat of spar varnish. Rub this down when dry, and apply the dull varnish over this.)

ALL UNITS FOR CHAIR EXCEPT SIDEPOSTS

The first method is to pick up a thin wash of color and medium on one part of your brush with a thicker mixture at the tip. Apply the wash with a generous sweeping movement of the brush, following the contour of the fruit or flower being tinted, leaving the heavier color on the shadowed side. Do not touch up. Wipe off entirely if poorly done.

Sometimes the colored wash is applied only to the part of the flower or fruit in shadow, so that a flower may be pure silver shadowed in blue, or gold shadowed in crimson, while leaves may be of a different shade of gold, shadowed in yellowish-green in their darker parts only. A basket or urn in such a combination would be shadowed in burnt umber.

The second method, for a very even color effect, is to dip brush in turpentine and squeeze out between pages of phone book. Dip in varnish, not wiping on the can. Brush it out on slick magazine. Apply varnish in long strokes to motif. Wipe out brush between magazine pages, so it is flat and square. Now, dip just the tip in varnish and then in the color desired. Brush out on paper so that there is hardly any color in the brush. Now dab it onto the wet varnish motif very lightly so that just a little color shows. In a few minutes the dabs will blend into one color area.

VIII. *Stenciling on light backgrounds*

It is necessary, on light backgrounds, to plan the arrangements of your stencil units before stenciling, so that a dark area the correct size and shape may be painted on the article to receive the bronze stenciling. Select the units which will make up the design and make a trial stencil, or several trial stencils, on a sample piece of black tin or cardboard. Be careful to leave only enough open space between units to represent their shadows. When the arrangement is as you wish it, trace an outline of the space which the design fills. Transfer this traced outline to the chair, or whatever you plan to stencil, by the usual methods already described in Chapter 3, pages 26–29. Paint this area in with a mixture of black oil color with varnish, with black Serviceseal (which should be used very sparingly because it spreads), or with some other dark color such as purple if special background effects are desired for special types of fruit.

When the painted area is tacky, apply the units as in any stenciling, exactly as you have originally placed them in the trial work.

Leaves may be traced around the stencil pattern when it is thoroughly dry. In traditional work, as on country yellow furniture, olive green was usually the color used. Tendrils, of the Palmer penmanship method variety, usually surrounded fruit patterns of this type, and veins were painted in the leaves to match them. These were done in black or semitransparent brown, and two stripes—the outer one black, the inner one either burnt sienna or burnt umber—completed the decoration.

IX. *Other combinations of painting and stenciling*

There are numerous uses for paint in connection with stenciling. Very often fine painted lines of yellow or black wove together a design composed of dark olive-green leaves with yellow veins and tips combined with stenciling in several shades of gold and copper. They arch in and out of the design, reappearing from behind units of the design and sometimes tapering off to nothing. Fine lines are also painted in many extremely fine curlicues around stenciled patterns showing leaves, fruit, or flowers. Sometimes they are formally done in very fine gold with a fine pen, at other times in bolder fashion in black or yellow with a small brush. It is well for such color touches to be repeated somewhere, as in a stripe around the edge of a piece.

Sometimes small details, such as the veins in leaves, or the stem of a bunch of grapes, are painted on a stenciled pattern. Attractive highlights may be added to grapes by touching each with a dot of yellow paint. The leaves in such a stencil would be veined in yellow. Sometimes, a stripe is painted on a classic urn or cornucopia in yellow; the details of birds, such as the eye and wing, are outlined with paint, the centers of flowers are outlined, or stamens dotted in. A familiar small sunburst on the rail of Hitchcock chairs usually has two elliptical lines painted over it in yellow. Two handsome chairs in the Essex Institute in Salem, stenciled over imitation walnut grain, have the design, which is one of fruit flowing from a cornucopia, somewhat outlined in black to make it stand out on its light background.

An old tray in the Harrison Gray Otis house in Boston has a very set stenciled border composed of a variety of motifs, some tinted. Along each side, the open center part of the tray has a spray of finely painted green leaves added to the stenciled border.

Almost any variety of combination of the two techniques may be found if you look far enough, so if your fancy leads you to invent your own combinations, there is plenty of precedent for doing so.

X. *The care of stencils*

> *Materials:* Painter's thinner, turpentine, Carbona or benzene
> Soft cloth or piece of absorbent cotton

You should treat your stencils with the greatest of care. When you are through using them, they are usually sticky with varnish and have bronze powder clinging to them as well. The latter could easily ruin subsequent stenciling if not carefully removed. Using a soft cloth and some form of solvent (above), wipe toward the cutout portion of the stencil, in order not to injure the edges of the design, until the stencil is clean. Reverse the linen and clean the other side. Stencils are easily stretched out of shape, so be careful not to pull the material as you clean it.

Stencils sometimes become torn, but it is possible to repair them if there is space to apply scotch tape. Apply it to both sides of the linen, for it needs to be strong to resist the pull of the sticky varnish.

It is an excellent idea to black large envelopes while you are using black paint for other purposes. Then, when you use a stencil for the first time, varnish an envelope at the same time, and after using your stencil on a chair or tray, apply the design to the envelope. It does not have to be applied in the proper relationship of parts, but can be easily recognized by its separate units. It is a good idea when tracing a stencil to save the tracing of the completed work and to enclose it in this same envelope so that you may refresh your mind on the details of its arrangement. Another type of envelope in which small stencils might be kept is the transparent sandwich bag.

These envelopes may be kept in an accordion-style manila filing case, under various headings, such as fruit, pictorials, flowers, borders, and so on.

Child's Chair in Natural Wood, with
Panel Cut to fit Stencil Pattern

VEINS

STENCIL FOR A CHILD'S CHAIR

Stencil from a child's applewood chair with cornucopia-shaped back slat

Cut separate stencil patterns for the apple, curving lines for blossom end of apple, melon, three different leaves for center, band for mouth of cornucopia, two leaves for cornucopia, convex for veins, two narrow lines with dots between, circle of dots with star. (Harrison Gray Otis House, Boston, Mass., Courtesy Society for the Preservation of New England Antiquities).

Varnish the piece and dry until tacky. Stencil the cornucopia rim in rich gold bronze. Use rich gold for stenciling fruit, shading as noted. Add details to apple with separate stencil, using pale gold lining bronze. Stencil leaves with pale gold lining, leaving center rib and veins in shadow. Large center leaves are placed first. Stencil veins in shadows by placing convex curved bit of linen where vein is to go and rubbing velvet around edge of curve. Stencil top leaf of cornucopia in pale gold, then lower leaf. Stencil bands, star, dots, and the like in rich gold. Stencil all veins on cornucopia by means of curved piece of linen, as above.

When thoroughly dry, varnish and dry again. Outline edge of cornucopia band (after rubbing down varnish) and edge of leaves (those shown with heavy line), with black tube paint and medium, applied with fine #1 pointed quill brush.

Paint (6) on head and seat rail of this chair in pale gold bronze mixed with medium. When only slightly tacky, apply gold leaf according to directions. If you do not desire to use gold leaf, brush additional pale gold bronze onto design while tacky. Finish chair as directed in Chapter 10.

Varied chair trims
for Hitchcock chairs and rockers

1. Painted design for the side posts of a fine Hitchcock chair. (Courtesy of the Society for the Preservation of New England Antiquities.) Paint the top section in pale gold bronze. When nearly dry, apply lemon gold leaf, or dust on dry gold bronze. Allow to dry. Wash off excess bronze. Varnish the side posts. Dry. Apply veins and double black lines in black with #1 quill brush. Paint the leaf design below in matching gold with #2 quill brush. Apply gold leaf or bronze to match previous decoration.

2. Painted motif for top of side posts, in gold bronze. When nearly dry, brush on dry bronze. Dry thoroughly, wash off excess gold, and varnish. Rub down. Paint two narrow stripes in old yellow outside the decoration.

3. Stenciled motif for seat rail (or for top rail if enlarged) of delicately stenciled chair. May be painted in gold bronze, if desired, instead of stenciling.

4. Same.

5. Stenciled border to trim ends of main slat of Hitchcock chair.

6. Stenciled border (cut from the edge of a strip of architect's linen) to trim ends of main splat of Hitchcock chair.

7. Design for seat rail (or for top rail if enlarged) of Hitchcock chair. Design is stenciled, then varnished. Fine lines in center are painted in old yellow with #1 quill brush.

8. Medallions. (Courtesy Essex Institute.) This type of medallion was frequently used at the end of curve on the top piece of certain kinds of rockers.

9. Design suitable for painting or stenciling on the seat rail (or top rail if enlarged) of Hitchcock chair.

10. Stenciled or painted motif for center part of side posts of Hitchcock chair.

VARIED CHAIR TRIMS

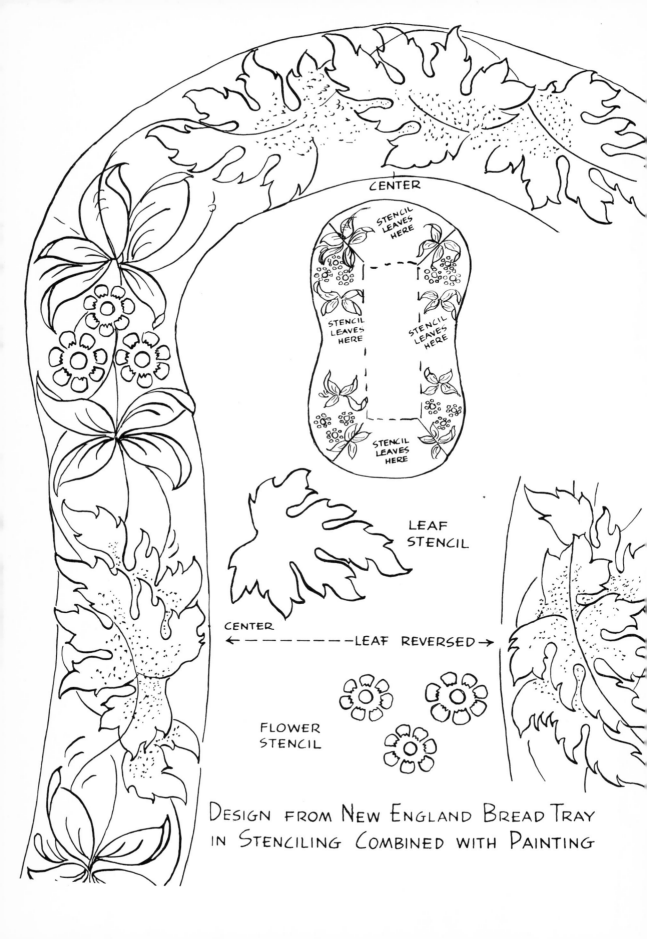

CENTER

STENCIL
LEAVES
HERE

STENCIL
LEAVES
HERE

STENCIL
LEAVES
HERE

STENCIL
LEAVES
HERE

LEAF
STENCIL

CENTER ←– – – – – –– –LEAF REVERSED→

FLOWER
STENCIL

DESIGN FROM NEW ENGLAND BREAD TRAY
IN STENCILING COMBINED WITH PAINTING

New England bread tray, stenciled and painted

This is a very attractive informal pattern suitable to a large variety of articles, including tables, boxes, picture frames, and chests. (Courtesy Essex Institute, Salem, Massachusetts).

First, plan where the group of three stenciled leaves should be repeated in the border. Decide whether the painted group of leaves will be used once, or repeated, between the principal groups of stenciled leaves. The flowers are often used right next to the three stenciled leaves as in the painted pattern of this type, (1) on page 87.

1. Stenciling. *Stencil the center leaf of a group in pale gold bronze, after varnishing the border and letting it dry until tacky. Stencil all the tips brightly, leaving only the center vein area and the center base of the leaf indistinct. Stencil very lightly around a curved bit of linen for the center vein. Stencil the leaf on the left in the same way, with a mixture of brilliant fire and antique copper bronze, showing only about three-fourths of the leaf, as the center one is supposed to shadow the other two. Stencil the leaf on the right in rich gold bronze. Next, stencil the flowers solidly in silver. Allow to dry 24 hours, or until thoroughly dry. Varnish and rub down with pumice and water.*

2. Painting. *Trace in the painted leaves and brush strokes. Paint them a deep olive green. Allow to dry 12 hours. Trace in the curving fine lines which lace through the pattern, the tips of leaves which are curled, and the veins in the painted leaves. Using a #1 pointed quill brush, paint these veins as finely as possible in country yellow. Paint the curving lines in pale gold bronze with medium (as in the original) or in country yellow. (They are done both ways on antique pieces.) When this is thoroughly dry, paint a very fine stripe with a fine striping brush very close to the border, on either side, in rich gold bronze. The original tray had a quarter-inch gold stripe around the floor of the tray.*

C H A P T E R

Painting natural flowers and fruits

I. *Flower painting*

The primary quality which sets flower painting apart is the necessity of depicting light and transparency. You must keep your strokes very light, gray your colors with a bit of raw umber or of contrasting color, since pure bright colors do not seem light and transparent; avoid working colors too much when wet, or they will appear too solid; paint leaves naturally *around* the flowers, not vice versa.

1. *Applying basic undercoats*

First, trace the outline of the flowers. (Leaves are merely sketched in, as they may need to be changed later.) Within this outline, apply a very smooth coat of white or the correct pale color, mixed with medium. Brush this on in smooth parallel strokes, quickly applied so that no brush marks show. Let this dry. Next, apply a coat of the approximate background color of the flower, half being darker than the rest to indicate shadow.

2. *Finishing the flower petals*

As you work, keep beside you some good color photos or reproductions of good paintings of the kind of flower you are painting. Postcards and seed catalogues are helpful in this respect. The main thing to remember from this point on in your painting is that the lightness and transparency of flowers can only be caught in paints by the lightest touch of the brush. Small delicate flowers, particularly, call for many tiny light strokes of the brush rather than heavy applications of paint. Another point to remember is that once these strokes have been applied they must not be worked over and over while wet, lest the pigment separate from the oil.

The darker parts of the flowers are always worked in before the highlights, usually with transparent colors such as Prussian blue, yellow lake or alizarin crimson. Wash transparent color on, graying by the addition of raw umber if it is required. For the lighter parts of the flower, thin the wash greatly with medium. In painting these shadows, remember that shadows are not always simply a darker shade of the flower or other object being painted. For example, white flowers are likely to have green or yellow-green shadows; blue flowers may have deeper blue shadows, or violet, gray, or even deep rose shadows; yellow flowers may be shadowed in burnt sienna or burnt umber. The shadows in the deep center of the flower are darkest of all. Do not work over this coat too much, and set aside to dry completely when finished.

Mix very faint color for the transition parts of the flower between highlight and shadow, graying it slightly with raw umber or with its contrasting color where necessary. Apply with the lightest strokes, with a small pointed quill brush, adding more white to your mixed color as it emerges from darker center to highest highlights. Do not work over this excessively while wet, although you will be tempted to do so since perfection always seems to be so far away when trying to bring nature down to a flat surface. Finally, while this paint is still wet, deftly apply highlights in pure white or a very light color with extremely fine light strokes. Set the work aside to dry before you are tempted to do more to it.

When the flowers are complete, trace or draw in the leaves and stems. They should not be an obvious part of the design, but should set off the flowers and be so arranged as to give a good contour to the entire design. Add or eliminate them in any traced design as necessary and subdue their colors so that they do not dominate the design.

3. *Suggestions for colors used in flower painting*

   A. White flowers

   > *Background:* Two coats Phillips white. Shade from medium green centers (with tinge of yellow) through transparent yellow-green into yellowish white to white.
   > *Stamens:* Yellow dots, sometimes with brown

   B. Light blue flowers

   > *Background:* One coat Phillips white, one coat pale blue
   > *Transparent coat:* Grayed Prussian blue, darker in the shadows. Shade from dark grayed blue through lighter grayed blue into white; or from red-violet through violet and blue into white.
   > *Stamens:* Dark blue, yellow, brown, or white

   C. Yellow flowers

   > *Background:* One coat Phillips white, one coat pale yellow

Transparent coat: Very thin wash of gamboge or Indian yellow, darker in the shadows. Shade from burnt umber through burnt sienna and dark orange into yellow and ivory highlights.

Stamens: Brown

D. Pink flowers (other than roses)

Background: One coat Phillips white, one coat light pink

Transparent coat: Alizarin crimson, darkest in shadows. Shade from alizarin crimson darkened with burnt umber through rose to pale pink and white. Shadows are sometimes blue, shading through violet into pink.

Stamens: Yellow, brown, or black

I. Eighteenth-century Floral Design

This design, drawn from an old piece of porcelain, may be painted in any colors that you desire. The rose may be pale yellow, shading to burnt umber in its shadows. The parrot tulip might then be violet with orange-tipped petals and orange side-petals. The daisies on the left may be blue with yellow centers, the flowers at top center transparent white, shading to pale yellow in the shadows, the bell-shaped flower violet-blue. The full-blown flower on the right may be dark brown, surrounded by petals of a deep gold color, shading to burnt umber.

Large leaves are painted with oxide of chromium green with a touch of raw umber. The veins are darkest green or brown. Small leaves vary from medium green to lighter gray-green. (Chapter 9 will give you guidance in painting the flowers.)

II. A Medallion of Roses

Paint the roses in natural pink, with transparent white painted over the petals. The leaves are dark green with brown or yellow veins. For an unusual effect, you may paint them gray-green, and when tacky brush them with silver or pale gold bronze powder. (See directions for free-hand bronzing, pp. 70–71.) The scrolls are painted with gold or silver bronze mixed with medium, and may afterward be accented with burnt umber. Or, on a light background, the scrolls may be painted in burnt umber.

EIGHTEENTH-CENTURY FLORAL DESIGN FOR A
ROUND BOX OR TRAY

E. Violet flowers

> *Background:* One coat Phillips white, one coat mauve
> *Transparent coat:* Violet with bluer tinge in shadows.
>   Shade from burnt umber center into grayed blue-vio-
>   let through blue up to pale pink highlights.
> *Stamens:* Pink, white, or yellow

II. *Fruit painting*

Begin painting a fruit with the darkest parts. Gradually work from these up to the highest highlights. When you have painted a little while, set the work aside and allow to dry. Add further touches 24 hours later. Use transparent oil color, washed on with a large brush, in one wide stroke if possible, to give effect of bloom on the fruit. If several strokes are used, blowing on the work at once will help the strokes to unite. Veil the transparent color, when dry, with a coat of opaque color, greatly thinned.

Study color photographs of fruit, or fine paintings of fruit, very closely. Practice modeling all kinds of fruit in paint, working from deepest shadow to lightest highlight.

Floral group suitable for a tray, silver chest, or box

The author has painted this design on an old oval tray as described below, but any color scheme may be used.

The roses are a very deep rose pink, the left one darker. The flowers above the deepest rose are pale blue, deeper blue in the center. The rosebud at left is deep pink. The rosebud at the right of the blue flowers is medium rose color. On its right are small greenish-white five-petaled flowers with darker green centers. Topmost flower is pale orange-yellow. The flower at the right of the entire group is pale blue, like those in the left upper group. The fuchsia is flame-red with violet petals and red stems and stamens. A bunch of tiny pale yellow flowers is just below the dark green leaves of the roses. These leaves are deep olive green with dark brown veins and shadows. The long narrow leaves surrounding the pattern are green, shaded in burnt umber. The leaves above the fuchsia are medium oxide of chrome green. The leaves nearer the top are lightest in color.

The author's tray is bordered in a fine gold-leaf scroll design which is shaded in burnt umber. This is on the floor of the tray, with a narrow gold stripe next to it. A wider stripe edges the tray.

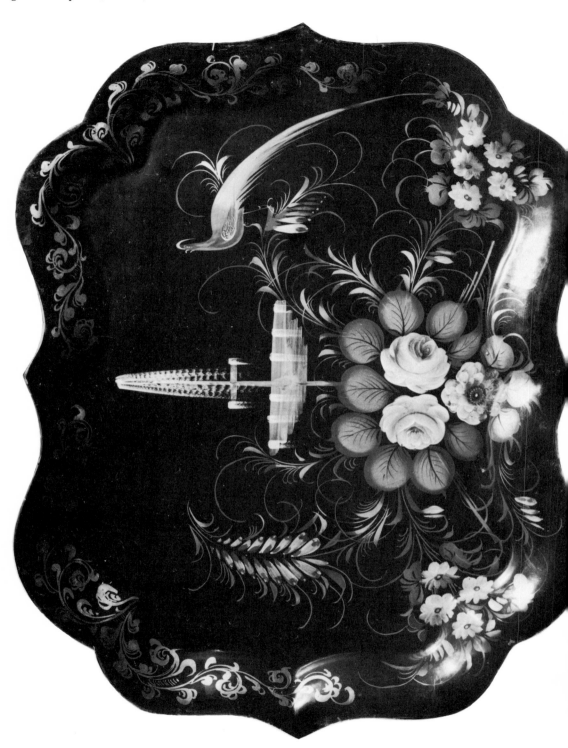

CHIPPENDALE TRAY WITH BIRD AND FLOWERS

Chippendale tray with a fountain and roses

The fountain, leaves, and bird are stylized, as are the drooping buds and corner flowers, while the roses are realistic. The design illustrated is one-half actual size. (Harrison Gray Otis House, Boston, Mass.)

1. **Prepare the black background according to directions in Chapter 1.** Arrange the two lower corner groups of flowers to fit the size and shape of your tray, and trace the design.

2. **Rose on right:** *paint inside the outlines of the entire left rose in pale pink, two coats. When dry, apply dark shadows in alizarin crimson, with a little Venetian red added. (See later directions for completing rose.)*

3. **Rose on left:** *paint it white, two coats. Apply shadow areas with a mixture of alizarin crimson, gamboge, and burnt umber. (See later directions also.)*

4. **Lowest flower with stylized overlapping transparent white petals:** Top half of flower: *swirl a #3 pointed quill brush through some permalba or titanium white which has been thinned out with medium on your palette. Then swirl the very tip of brush through some thicker white. Beginning with the outer row of petals, form each petal with a circular sweep of the brush, depositing a film of the thicker white on the rim of the petal.*

Lower half of flower: *its general effect is transparent gray, so thin your white more than above, and pick up only a little extra white on tip of brush. Apply petals as above.*

Center area: *wash this area with a mixture of transparent gamboge and a touch of Prussian blue, making an olive-green center. The smaller center is Venetian red, as is the outer row of dots. When Venetian red dries, apply a circle of yellow dots inside the reddish brown dots, made of chrome yellow medium with white. In the center of the Venetian red center is a yellow dot.*

5. **Silvered leaves:** *paint large leaves gray-green, one coat. When dry, apply a second coat. Leave this until tacky and brush silver (chromium bronze) from the center of the leaf gradually outward, with a soft paintbrush or velvet, letting the silver fade out gradually to green edges. (See Chapter 3.)*

6. **Small groups of flowers in corners:** *paint pale blue, two coats. (See later details for completing.)*

148

7. Leaves around these flowers: *gray-green, but do not apply silver.*

8. Completing rose on right: *work up the petals of the rose with a mixture of transparent alizarin crimson and white, applied with a fat #3 pointed quill brush, its tip swirled through a little extra white, almost pure. Apply in a swirling motion, leaving extra white on the edge of the petals where they curl back slightly (indicated by petal lines). Wipe off unsatisfactory attempts and try again if necessary.*

When first petals are dry, use a #2 pointed quill brush and lightly touch the inside of the petals with a wash of alizarin crimson, using deeper crimson for the underside of petals. Add a little burnt umber to the crimson for the depths of the rose.

Using a fine brush, a very light touch, and very thinned-out white, apply in a filmy transparent coat with tiny strokes to each petal. Pick up a very little extra white on the tip of the brush and define the edges of a few filmy petals beyond the perimeter of the rose already made— mere suggestions of petals.

Add about four yellow dots in center.

9. Completing rose on left: *work up the petals in the same way as the other rose, picking up a wash of gamboge for the deeper parts of the petals, shading into a curling edge of white on each petal. Allow to dry.*

Work darker shadows in transparent yellow with a touch of burnt umber added. The center is alizarin crimson with a touch of burnt umber and gamboge.

Finally, as on the other rose, paint on a very wispy transparent coat of white with tiny strokes and a fine brush, so that it is not apparent that it is separately applied. Define a few suggestions of petal edges just outside the edge of the rose.

10. Fountain: *the bowl of the fountain is painted with long horizontal strokes in a mixture of transparent yellow (gamboge or Indian yellow) with a little white. When dry, the left side of the fountain (in shadow) is shaded with a thin wash of burnt umber. The upper level of the fountain is painted the same way. The base of the fountain is also yellow.*

11. Water: *the center column of water is painted in long transparent strokes of white. The spray falling from the top is begun with a rather dry brush of white, enough to make a slight opaque stroke at the top. The brush is dry enough, however, that as you draw it downward it only*

149

*makes an intermittent impression of transparent white, like water fall-
ing unevenly. Complete the entire cascade with one stroke, if possible,
diminishing the amount of paint applied as your brush descends. The
thin wisps of water falling outward from the top are fine lines of transparent white, also drawn out on a fine brush, rather dry.*

*The eight cascades of water falling from the two levels of the fountain
are begun with a fairly solid stroke of white, diminishing rapidly to the dry-
brush intermittent technique. (This veiled quality of transparent white
paint over black cannot be conveyed in a black-and-white drawing, but
you must practice to achieve the lacy effect of water with an almost dry
brush, leaving a film of water only where the water first spurts from
the fountain.)*

12. The bird: *paint the body in transparent white strokes, tapering
off to nothing for tail feathers, with a dry brush. (A certain streaked-
ness is permissible, as white was seldom applied evenly, except in natural flowers.) When dry, paint the body with a wash of alizarin crimson
in a rose-red value, except for wing and head, which are dark alizarin.
Taper these strokes off unevenly near the wing area. Allow to dry.*

Tail feathers: *picking up transparent yellow (gamboge or Indian
yellow) on the brush, with a little white added, draw the brush out into
long, dry, wispy strokes for tail feathers, covering the white tail feathers,
and adding new transparent ones. Beware of making these too opaque.*

Wing decorations, head details, and feet: *using a #1 pointed quill
brush held vertically, apply these lines with the finest of strokes in white.
They may even be added with a croquille pen and water- and varnishproof white ink.*

13. Sprays of leaves, curving stems, and curving lines: *paint all these
gray-green. While paint is still tacky, brush chromium bronze on all
the leaves, sprays, and lines, as instructed in Chapter 3. Leave larger
leaves green at the base. Brush lightly toward edges, leaving green showing. Smaller leaves are silvered except at tips. Fine curving lines and
stems are largely silver.*

14. Drooping buds: *four lower groups of oval buds.*

Group of three on left: *paint in semitransparent white. Allow to
dry. Shade from deep alizarin crimson on shadow side through faint
pink to white. Dry. Paint tops oxide of chrome green with white and
raw umber added.*

Group of four on lower left: *paint and shade in same way. When dry, add oval blob at bottom in medium value of alizarin crimson, and tops of same green as above.*

Group of two on right: *paint transparent white only.*

Group of three on lower right: *paint transparent white. When dry, add green top and crimson blob, as above.*

Upper groups of drooping buds: Left upper group: *all of these are painted first in transparent white and allowed to dry. The three-lobed tip is painted with a mixture of alizarin crimson and Venetian red. A dot of yellow is added when the red is dry. Tops are oxide of chrome green with a little white added.*

Right upper group of buds below the bird: *paint the two largest buds with transparent white and allow to dry. Paint the oval blob at the tip alizarin crimson. Paint the four smaller buds first in white and allow to dry. Wash with alizarin crimson to give a rose color. Paint all the tops with oxide of chrome green, mixed with a little white and a speck of raw umber. Add a yellow dot to the tip of each bud.*

15. Groups of flowers in lower corners: *apply daisy petals in white, two coats if necessary. When dry, shade the lower and outer sides of these flowers with a wash of Prussian blue, merging naturally into the white. The oval centers are Venetian red. Add a tiny yellow center dot when dry. Small drops from these flowers are first painted white, then washed with Prussian blue when dry. The rounded shapes above the center daisy of right group were transparent white with green at their base (but they could be turned into green leaves). The groups of leaves around the blue daisies are oxide of chrome green, mixed with white and raw umber. Shade when dry with burnt umber on the shadow side. Vein with burnt umber.*

16. Two groups of buds on lower edge, either side of center group of flowers: *those on the left are white, with oxide of chrome green tops, mixed with white and raw umber. Those on the right are painted white, allowed to dry, then washed in a mixture of alizarin crimson and Venetian red. Apply a dot of yellow at the lower tips. The top of the bud is the same green as the other buds.*

17. *Complete the tray with a scroll pattern around the top and sides. (Shown full size on pages 152–153.) Paint in a medium shade of gold bronze. When tacky, brush on additional gold bronze to give a burnished-gold look. The original scrolls were unshaded, but burnt umber shading is recommended.*

:(PATTERN FULL SIZE)

Design For Trim o
Chippendale Tray
with Fountain

TOP

152

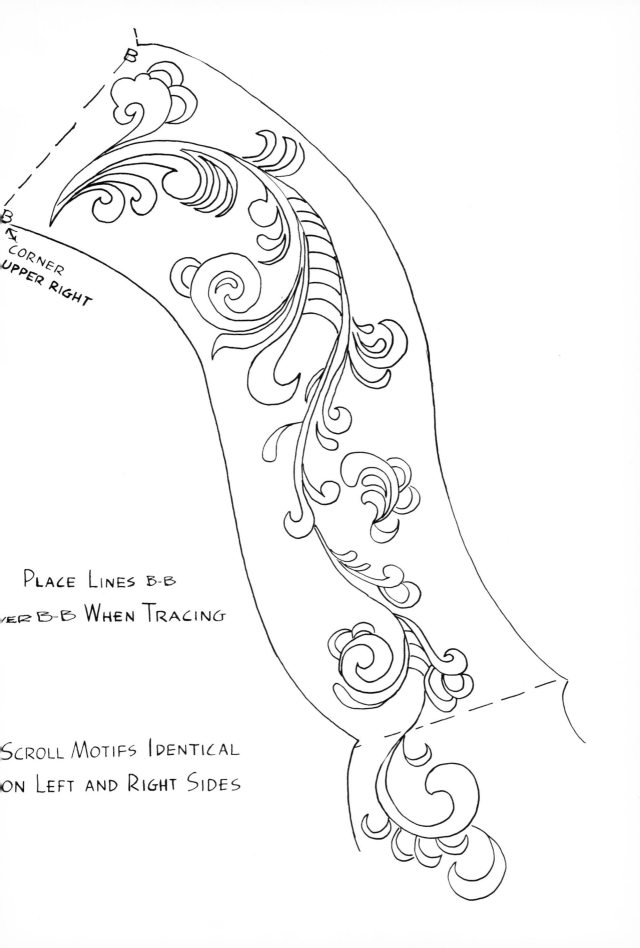

CORNER
UPPER RIGHT

PLACE LINES B-B
OVER B-B WHEN TRACING

SCROLL MOTIFS IDENTICAL
ON LEFT AND RIGHT SIDES

Lace-edge Tray

These simple flowers are of a distinct technique, found only on trays of the late eighteenth and early nineteenth century as a rule, and almost always on those with a pierced gallery which sometimes flares outward at the edge. The flowers are closely allied to peasant painting in shape, but have a transparent look. The illustration is one-half actual size.

Method: background black, or tortoise-shell effect if desired. (See Chapter 2.) Varnish background and rub down according to background instructions.

Paint round fruit and flowers, (1) and (2), solidly with cadmium red light (mixed with medium) using a showcard brush or a fat #3 or #4 pointed quill brush and smooth straight strokes. Use two coats if they are required to cover the black well. Allow to dry thoroughly.

1. Fruit: *mix several batches of color on your palette so that the fruit (2) can be shaded from rather a dark red through light red, into soft yellow and yellowish-white highlights at lightest point of upper fruit.*

> Dark red: *cadmium red light, with a touch of alizarin crimson and burnt umber*
> Light red: *cadmium red light.*
> Soft yellow: *chrome yellow, white, and touch of raw umber*
> Yellowish-white: *same, with white predominating*

Paint upper fruit first, shading as naturally as possible from dark to light by the use of light feathery strokes when merging colors, and by the addition of a little of the lighter colors to the dark where the change comes. Toward the top of the shaded section the fruit begins to turn yellow. The highest, whitest highlight is at the top right of the fruit. Allow to dry thoroughly. Do not work over too often or you will cause the colors to separate from their oils.

When the first fruit is dry, shade the lower fruit from the same dark red through light red, with just a hint of yellow in its upper right portion. (It is shadowed by the upper fruit.)

2. Stems: *paint with permalba or titanium white thinned with medium to semitransparency.*

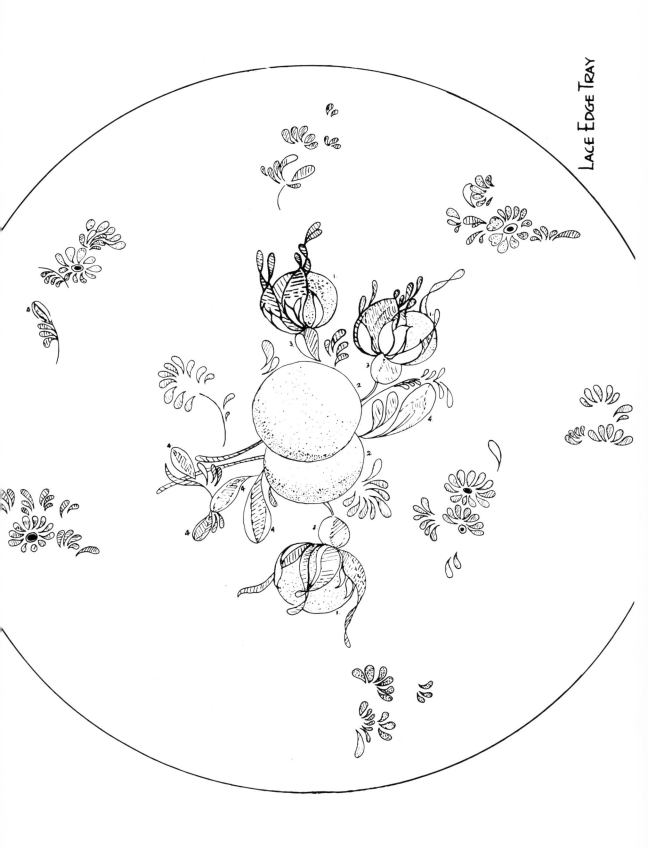

3. Parts 3 and 4: *using a fat pointed brush, pick up a good deal of thinned white on the brush. Then swirl one side of the brush under a dab of white paint, so that the brush holds two values of white. Paint these parts with a swirling motion of the brush, pressing the transparent side of the brush down first and swirling the heavier white on, where indicated white, with the later part of the stroke.*

4. Rose petals: *using white thinned with medium, paint the transparent white petals (those marked with parallel lines). Using a #3 pointed quill brush, paint them in brush-stroke technique (see Chapter 4) You may highlight the upper tips of some of·the petals with a little heavier white if desired. Allow to dry.*

5. Leaves on roses: *paint leaves indicated as white with an opaque coat, using brush-stroke technique and highlighting somewhat.*

6. Lace edge: *if you are doing this pattern appropriately on an old lace-edge tray or a reproduction, varnish the lace edge and apply pale gold lining bronze with a velvet or brush, fading downward from solid gold at the top to nothing near bottom of the tray.*

7. Finishing: *varnish with several coats of varnish when entirely dry, using asphaltum for antique effect in the next-to-last coat. Rub down well between each two coats and after final coat. (See directions for finishing, pp. 157–160.)*

156

Finishing processes

The final steps *after* decorating are often those which give a piece a finished, mellow look in place of crude brightness.

First of all, an over-all coat of varnish must be applied to protect the decoration. Then various methods may be used to mellow the colors. The number of protective coats varies with the use to which the piece will be put. Two or three might suffice for an article to be used for decoration only. Never use less than five or six on a piece which is to be used for practical purposes. Dull or satin finish varnish is used only as a top coat, where heat resistance is not a desired feature.

I. Varnishing

  Materials: Best quality fresh bar varnish or spar varnish, such
       as Supervalspar or Wheeler's Bar Varnish
      A very fine, flexible varnish brush, 1½″ width, of
      oxhair or camel's hair, to be used *only* for varnish

157

Materials, Cont.: Turpentine for thinning
Newspapers

Use varnish only over paint which has dried thoroughly, allowing *at least* 24 hours to elapse after it feels dry. Varnishing should be done in a room heated to at least 75° F. Both object and varnish should be slightly warm. A kitchen is a good place in which to varnish, because it is likely to be easy to make dust-free, and can be warmed by opening the oven door. Varnish only on dry days, as humidity affects drying adversely. (Certain oils in varnish must evaporate before other oils dry and seal their stickiness in.)

Start with a clean brush, removing any loose hairs. Do not stir or shake the varnish can, nor wipe the brush on the edge of the can. Flow the varnish on in long straight strokes in one direction. (In varnishing a tray, varnish the outer sides first, then the inner sides, then the floor of the tray in lengthwise strokes. The back may be both painted and varnished later.) Brush out immediately any bubbles or drips which appear on the surface before they have time to set. If your brush has many bubbles in it, squeeze these out between folds of clean newspaper. Bubbles are caused by stirring or shaking varnish, by working the brush on the edge of the can, or by vigorous back-and-forth strokes of the brush. Ribbed varnish comes from varnishing with cold varnish, or thickened varnish.

Leave the varnished piece in a warm dust-free place to dry. It should not be rubbed down or have any painting done over it until at least 24 hours after it feels completely dry to the touch. Glossy spots will result if you rub down too soon.

II.   *Rubbing down the varnish coat*

All coats of varnish, except the final coat, which is always rubbed with oil and pumice (or rottenstone), are rubbed in one of the following ways.

1. *Pumice and water method*

>*Materials:* Fine dental-grade powdered pumice, or rottenstone
>Absorbent cotton or a piece of felt or heavy flannel

Purchase the finest powdered pumice from a drugstore. Rottenstone is another fine abrasive you may use. Wet the article to be rubbed and sprinkle pumice over it from a kitchen saltshaker. With a wad of absorbent cotton or a piece of felt, rub the entire surface, going over it lightly but firmly with a circular motion. Be careful not to scour through the varnish into the decoration or background. When washing the article in cold water reveals that the gloss has been evenly removed, the piece is ready for its next coat. Wash thoroughly with Ivory soap and warm water.

2. *Steel wool method*

>*Material:* #0000 steel wool

Take a wad of the specified steel wool. Use no water. Rub same as above. This is a good method to use if you are trying to rub down a ribbed varnish coat.

3. *Wet and dry sandpaper method*

>*Materials:* #0000 wet and dry sandpaper
>Ivory soap

This is a good method when you are trying to get rid of any bubbles in the varnish. Wet the paper and rub it on the soap. Then rub evenly all over the piece.

4. *Trimite paper*

>*Material:* Trimite paper

Trimite paper is a very fine abrasive, usually used dry, as is steel wool. Many people like to use it, but I prefer methods 1 and 2.

III.   *Rubbing down the final varnish coat*

> *Materials:* Crude oil or paraffin oil
> Fine dental-grade powdered pumice, or rottenstone
> Absorbent cotton, a piece of heavy woolen cloth such
> as flannel, or felt

The final varnish coat *follows* the use of one of the glazing methods described below, but the glazes may be omitted entirely. Allow any glaze to dry thoroughly before varnishing over it.

Sprinkle the piece which has been varnished, and allowed to dry well, with powdered pumice or rottenstone. Dip a wad of absorbent cotton or a piece of felt or woolen into crude oil or paraffin oil (obtainable at hardware stores), and rub it with the same painstaking circular motion used in applying pumice and water.

When the surface is satiny and evenly polished, wipe off surplus pumice and oil with a clean cloth until it is completely dry.

The article may be polished occasionally thereafter with crude oil, if it is much used. If it is for decorative purposes only, it may be waxed from time to time with good wax.

IV.   *Glazing and antiquing*

Glazes are made by using artist's oil colors, usually by adding small amounts to varnish, sometimes by adding them to a mixture of turpentine and raw linseed oil.

Blue glaze is attractive over gray, pale green over pale blue, dull blue over rose, vermilion over yellow (especially to make the interior of a dark piece brilliant), blue-green over violet.

Some glazes are known as *antiquing*. They cause the colors in the decoration to fade back as though time had mellowed them. Some methods for this follow.

1. *Antiquing with burnt umber or burnt sienna in varnish*

Add a very little burnt umber or burnt sienna tube oil color to one or more of the intermediate coats of varnish. A combination of burnt umber and burnt sienna may also be used. Rub down this varnish coat as above.

2. *Antiquing with asphaltum in varnish*

Adding asphaltum to spar varnish gives a very mellow look to antique pieces being restored, but does have a softening effect on varnish so that it scratches easily. Therefore use it *between other coats of varnish*, rather than next to your decoration or as a top coat. Rub it down more carefully than usual, as it is softer than straight varnish. Add only enough asphaltum (which is bought in cans at a hardware store) to the varnish to color it faintly.

3. *Antiquing with linseed oil and tube oil colors, on painted wood*

A linseed oil antiquing coat is used mostly over light backgrounds, and is applied unevenly to darken certain areas to make a piece look old.

Mix equal parts of raw linseed oil and turpentine with a little japan dryer. (Work in a well-ventilated room when using the japan dryer.) Prepare a dauber by wrapping a wad of absorbent cotton in a piece of stocking. Place some of this mixture in a saucer, and on the edge of the saucer place a little burnt umber or burnt sienna oil color (or any desired color). Dip your dauber into the mixture, then lightly into the color, and tamp the dauber lightly on the painted surface. Wipe the mixture toward the edges of the piece with the palm of your hand, into the crevices and grain of the wood. Let the color fade out at the edges of the piece. Tamp a little extra color around the central design if there is one. Remove surplus color with a clean wad from immediately around the design, and spread the rest of this color outward with the palm of your hand. Apply the color smoothly, not in streaks. Leave some natural highlights. Emphasize the decorating by using darker color around it, but do not use color over it.

The oil takes a long time to dry, sometimes a week or more. Varnish over it only when thoroughly dry.

4. *Antiquing with smoke*

Varnish the piece once. Rub it down. Varnish again. When this coat is just tacky—when the finger can just barely cling to the surface—hold the piece upside down over a smoking candle for a few seconds. The smoking may be uneven, but do not let the smoke get on the design. Varnish when dry. This looks well over country yellow pieces or those of orange color.

Never shellac over sticky paint or varnish in the belief that it will help it to dry. It creates its own slick surface over the sticky paint, but underneath the paint is still sticky. If the article is nicked or scratched, the sticky paint will smear.

11

Reverse painting on glass

Many old mirrors were decorated with paintings which show through a panel of clear glass above the mirror glass. Many of these were primitive paintings done in color. Others were painted in gold with dark details, or were done in gold leaf against a black background.

The design to be copied is fastened with Scotch tape to the right side of the glass. The inside of the glass is varnished with a good grade of clear varnish and allowed to dry 24 hours or more. The finest details of the design are painted *first* with a #1 or #2 pointed brush. Dip it in varnish, to which a few drops of turpentine have been added, then brush it in a little oil color, make a practice stroke, and apply the details. Allow to dry well. Apply shadows or small dark areas next, using a #3 brush. (Transparent colors such as burnt umber are often used for this.) Allow to dry well. Next, paint highlights on darker motifs. Allow to dry well, unless you wish them to be blended into the color they highlight, in which case that must be applied at once, watching the blending from the right side of the glass, too. When the highlights are dry, paint the solid motifs, using a #3 or #4 square-tipped showcard brush in most cases. Allow to dry well. A background color, usually made by tinting flat white to pale blue, gray, or bluish white, is applied with a larger square-tipped brush over the whole area. In the case of sky, this color is usually paler at the top. A second coat, when the first dries, will probably be needed. When it dries, varnish over it, to protect the painting.

If the painting is largely in gold bronze, varnish the glass as above. Details are first painted in black or in burnt umber, burnt sienna, or a mixture of the last two, using a #1 brush dipped in varnish to which has been added a drop or two of turpentine. Dry well. Shadows are painted in transparent color on the principal motifs. Dry well. The gold areas are finally painted with a #2 or #3 brush, which is first dipped in varnish and then in a good quantity of gold bronze powder. When this has dried almost completely, dust a little dry gold bronze over it with a soft brush, to prevent the gold from looking transparent or streaked.

Dutch tile designs

A design such as one of these found on old tiles can easily be adapted for decorating the top of an early American mirror. The line work is typical of the primitive painting done on some of these mirrors.

The designs illustrated (from the Metropolitan Museum of Art) could be painted in burnt umber or burnt sienna, or black. A pale blue or pale yellow background might be used.

Or the central motif might be applied in gold leaf, with the lines very finely drawn in dark brown or black.

Designs from Dutch Tiles

VERY PRIMITIVE DESIGN TO BE PAINTED ON THE REVERSE SIDE
of GLASS AT THE TOP OF A MIRROR

*Primitive design to be painted on the reverse side
of a piece of glass at the top of a mirror*

1. *Attach pattern face down to right side of piece of glass, with Scotch
tape. Paint all the fine black lines shown, except shading indicating
dark color of front door opening, using black oil color with medium
and a #1 pointed quill brush, mingling deeper red for shadow while
paint is wet. Paint fence dark burnt umber—also weed at bottom. Allow
to dry thoroughly.*

2. *Paint house light barn-red color; do not paint windows, roof, door,
or chimney yet. Paint tree trunk dark brown, mingling darker shade of
brown on shadow side while wet. Paint tree branches with single large
brush strokes, if possible, using #4 showcard brush, one edge of which
has been laid in darker green for underside of branches as medium
gray-green color is picked up on brush. Allow this much to dry thoroughly.*

*Beginning with shadows from trees for which burnt umber is used,
fill in hillside with oxide of chromium green, grayed with raw umber,
merging shadows with hillside background. Use broad strokes and fill
in as quickly as possible. Allow to dry.*

*Paint doorway and windows burnt umber; roof dark gray, deeper
near eaves; chimney very dark red. Paint pathway gray, merging into
burnt umber at side to indicate shadow. Allow to dry.*

*Paint in background of blue-white or blue-gray tint on top of all
previous painting. When thoroughly dry, varnish for protection.*

Alternate method in gold.

*Paint black lines, allow to dry. Add more black lines for shadow de-
tail on trees, road, and so forth. Using varnish or gold-size for house,
trees, and fence, apply gold leaf to varnish areas when varnish is tacky.
Varnish over gold leaf when thoroughly dry (at least 24 hours). Paint
hillside pale blue, shadow side of road slightly deeper tint. When hillside dries thoroughly, wash white background over entire piece. (Hillside may be deeper shade of gold leaf if desired, instead of pale color,
or house may be rich gold and hillside pale gold.) Gold bronzes mixed
with medium could be used, but would not have the same effect as gold
leaf.*

When it has dried at least 24 hours, extra bronze must be carefully brushed off, and any that remains must be carefully washed off with water and mild soap. The background is then applied with a larger square-tipped brush. This may be flat black, or one of the colors mentioned above, according to the effect desired. Dry. Coat with varnish.

If gold leaf is applied, details may be made either by etching the gold leaf after it is applied with a sharp tool so that the black background shows through, by painting them in with a tiny brush in one of the dark colors mentioned above, or by drawing them in with waterproof, varnishproof black India ink with a fine crow-quill pen. Varnish is applied to the glass as a first coat in any case. Allow to dry well. Unless etching is used, apply the details as above. Dry thoroughly. Varnish over all. Dry. Now apply varnish (or you may use gold-size, if preferred) to the gold motifs only. Dry to the stage at which your finger, touched to the varnish, *barely* adheres. Apply the gold leaf according to instructions on pages 82–83. If any errors are made in the gold leafing, extra bits which adhere must be removed *entirely,* with a bit of cotton on a toothpick which has been lightly dipped in carbon tetrachloride. If details are etched, etch them 24 hours after leafing. When leaf has dried several days, varnish over the entire surface, to protect it. Dry well. Apply flat black background, if that is the background desired, or one of the pale colors, as above.

If the painting is to be outlined with a gold, black, or colored stripe, remember that this must be applied *before* any of the design.

A portfolio of design material

The following portfolio is full of material from which you may choose and combine to make interesting designs of your own. The flowers and fruit do not necessarily have a close connection with those you find in nature, but will suggest to you many ways in which to use them. Naturally, the more stylized will combine best with each other, the more natural with those of the same type. Nature, however, often draws in bold strokes, in which case the natural and the stylized will harmonize in design.

The usefulness of this portfolio does not confine itself to painting and stenciling on wood and metal. The designs may just as well be used for embroidery or for painting and stenciling on fabric and paper.

Do not consider time wasted when you trace and combine and change these patterns. The more your hand becomes used to flowing design, the more easily you will be able to create original designs.

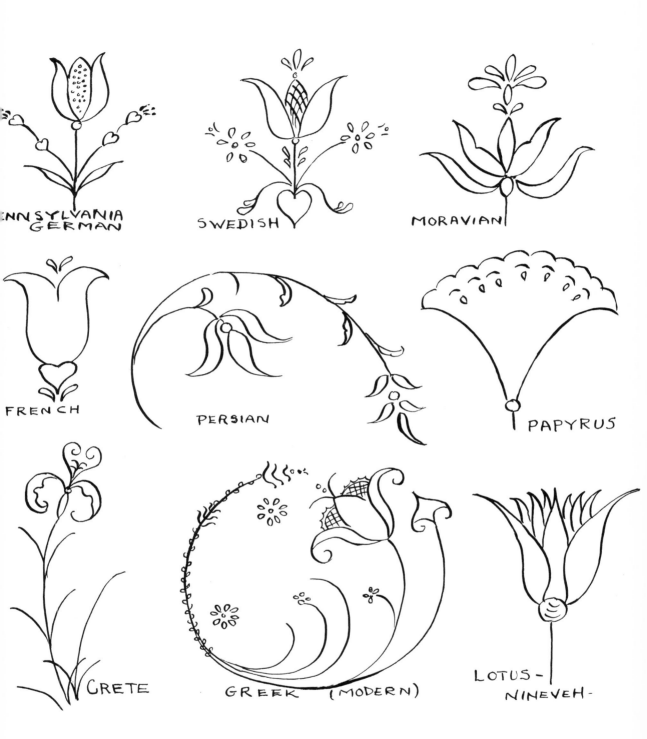

PENNSYLVANIA GERMAN

SWEDISH

MORAVIAN

FRENCH

PERSIAN

PAPYRUS

CRETE

GREEK (MODERN)

LOTUS-NINEVEH-

FLORAL PATTERNS
TULIPS AND OTHERS.

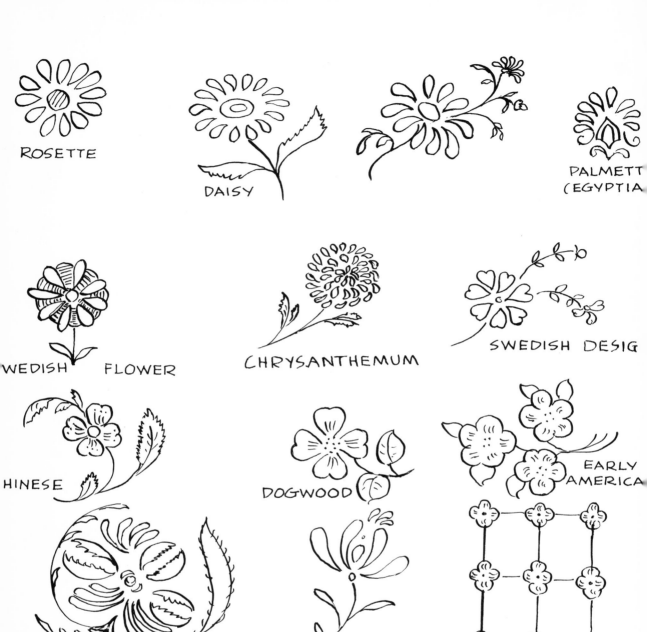

ROSETTE

DAISY

PALMETT (EGYPTIA

WEDISH FLOWER

CHRYSANTHEMUM

SWEDISH DESIG

HINESE

DOGWOOD

EARLY AMERICA

RUSSIAN

GERMAN

FRENCH

Floral Patterns —
Rosette and other shapes

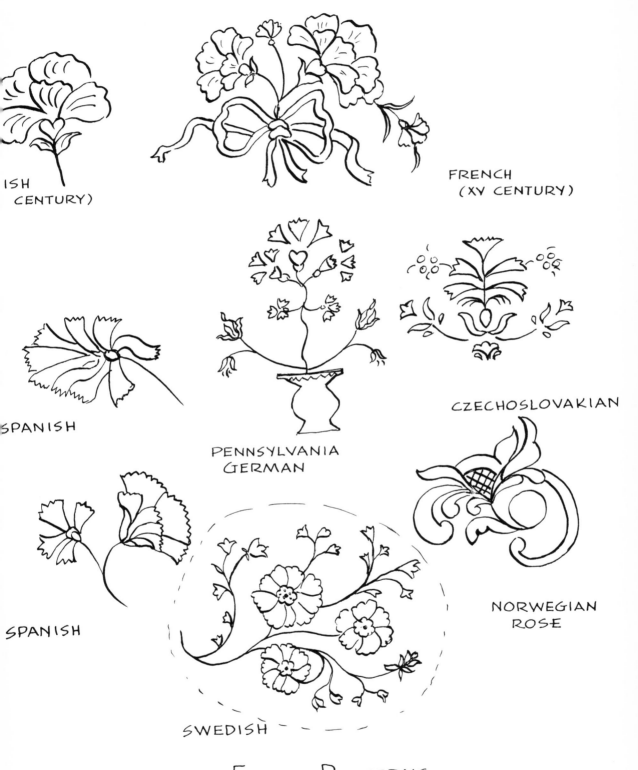

ISH
(CENTURY)

FRENCH
(XV CENTURY)

SPANISH

PENNSYLVANIA
GERMAN

CZECHOSLOVAKIAN

SPANISH

SWEDISH

NORWEGIAN
ROSE

FLORAL PATTERNS
CARNATIONS AND ROSE

173

ROSE -
NEW ENGLAND

WILD ROSE

ROSE
FREN

MORNING GLORY
ENGLISH

CZECHOSLOVAKIAN

BUD -
FRENCH

NORWEGIAN "ROSE - MAHLING"
(ROSE - PAINTING)

VIOLET

GERMAN

PANSY

STYLIZED ROSES AND FRILLY-PETALLED FLOWER

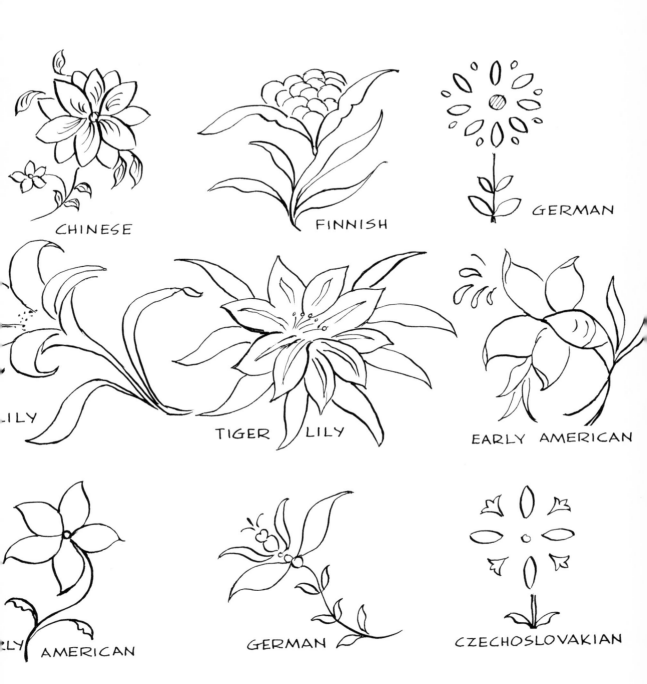

CHINESE

FINNISH

GERMAN

LILY

TIGER LILY

EARLY AMERICAN

AMERICAN

GERMAN

CZECHOSLOVAKIAN

LILY PATTERNS

175

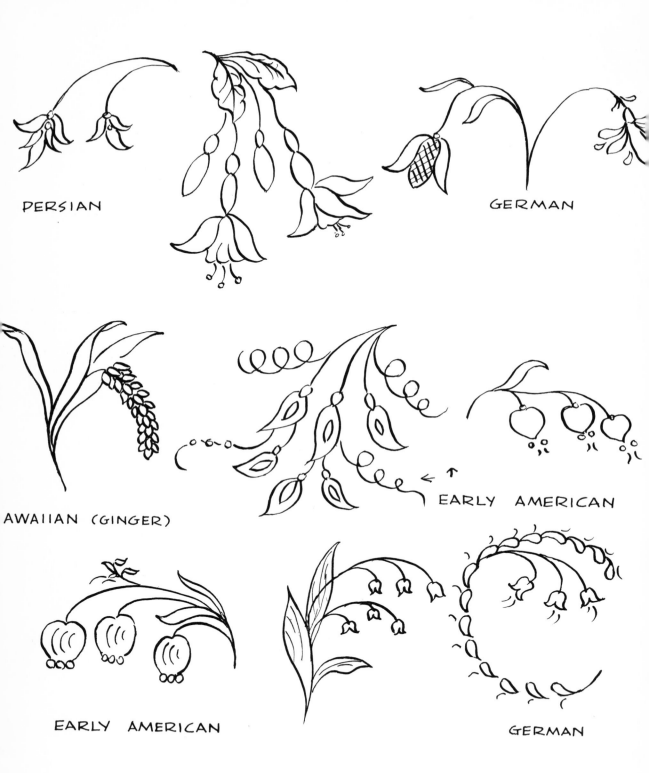

PERSIAN

GERMAN

AWAIIAN (GINGER)

EARLY AMERICAN

EARLY AMERICAN

GERMAN

Pendant Flowers

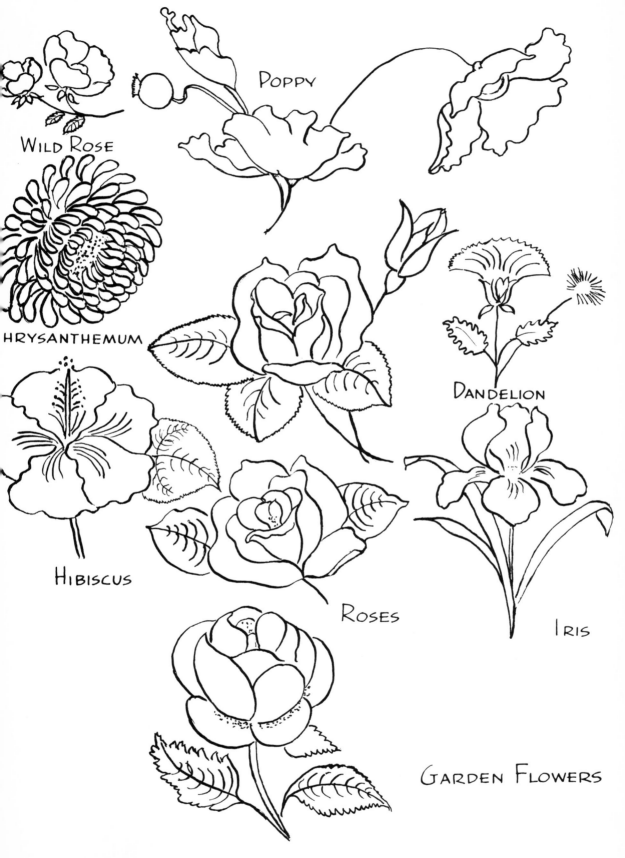

WILD ROSE

POPPY

CHRYSANTHEMUM

HIBISCUS

DANDELION

ROSES

IRIS

GARDEN FLOWERS

GUAVA

APPLE

CHERRY

QUINCE

GRAPE

STRAWBERRY

PEAR

APRICOT, PLUM, PEACH

ACORN

FRUITS

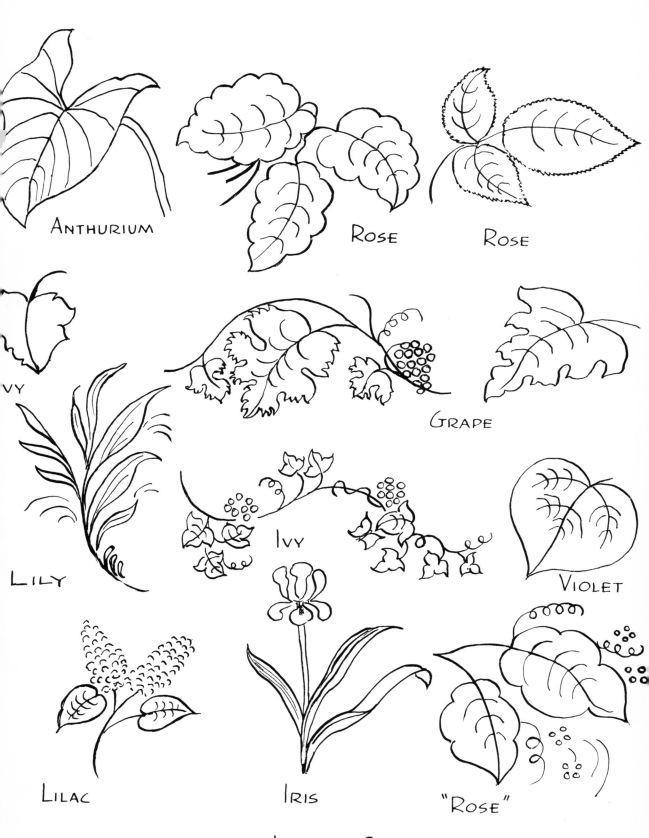

ANTHURIUM

ROSE

ROSE

IVY

GRAPE

LILY

IVY

VIOLET

LILAC

IRIS

"ROSE"

LEAVES - I

179

MAPLE

MAPLE

BEECH

OAK

OAK

TROPICAL
BREADFRUIT

BANANA

CANDLENUT

PHILODENDRON

OLIVE

HOLLY

LEAVES - II

180

CHINESE

CHINESE

CHINESE

SPANISH

CHINESE

CHINESE

PERSIAN

PENNSYLVANIA
GERMAN

BUTTERFLIES
AND MYTHICAL BEASTS

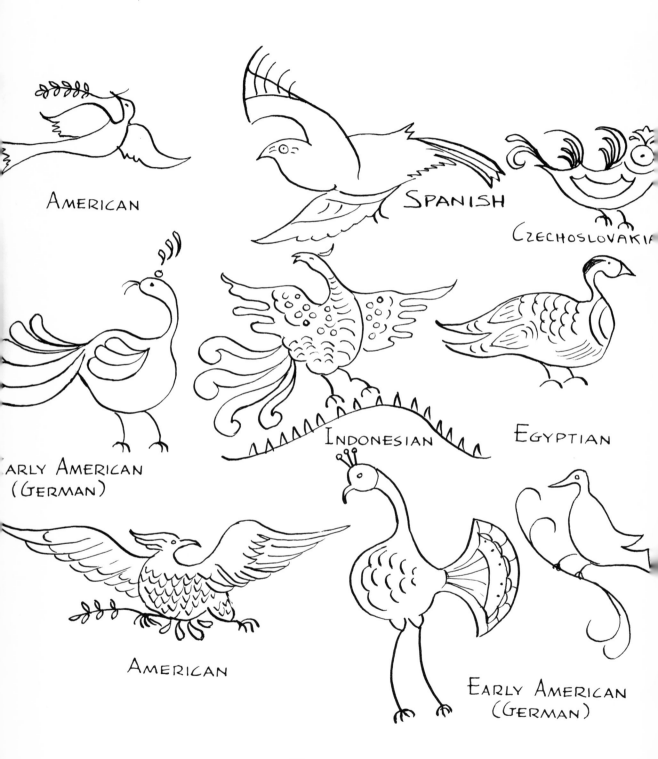

AMERICAN

SPANISH

CZECHOSLOVAKIA

EARLY AMERICAN
(GERMAN)

INDONESIAN

EGYPTIAN

AMERICAN

EARLY AMERICAN
(GERMAN)

BIRDS

CHINESE SCENES-I

183

CHINESE SCENES - II

Bibliography

Books

BRAZER, ESTHER. *Early American Decoration*. Springfield, Mass.: Pond-Ekberg Co., 1947. A well-illustrated book with photographs of a variety of painted and stenciled pieces, largely in the New England styles, with information on the author's techniques.

MURRAY, MARIA D. *The Art of Tray Painting*. New York: Studio Publications, 1954. A text abounding in photographs of painted trays, some quite elaborate.

ROBACHER, EARL F. *Pennsylvania Dutch Stuff*. Philadelphia. Pennsylvania University Press, 1944. A fairly complete book, devoted to all the Pennsylvania German crafts. Some illustrations, both in color and black and white, of painted pieces.

SMITH, JANET K. *Design, An Introduction*. New York: Prentice-Hall, Inc., 1946. A study of the theory of design. Good for its fine bibliography.

VANDERWALKER, F. N. *Mixing of Colors and Paints*. Wilmette, Ill.: Frederick J. Drake Co., 1939.

WARING, JANET. *Early American Stencil Decorations*. Watkins Glen, N.Y.: Century House, 1950. A complete and well-illustrated history of stenciling, including application to walls.

Booklets

DEVOE, SHIRLEY. *American Decorated Chairs.* New Milford, Conn.: Mock and Marsh, 1947. Description of types of painted and stenciled chairs, with their appropriate decoration.

DOWNS, JOSEPH. *Pennsylvania German Arts and Crafts Picture Book.* New York: Metropolitan Museum of Art, 1942. A small picture book with examples of a number of different crafts, including a few of interest to the painter.

HOKE, ELIZABETH S. *Pennsylvania German Painted Tin,* Home Craft Course, Vol. 5. Plymouth Meeting, Pa.: Mrs. C. N. Keyser, 1943. Authentic designs in black and white for small tinware.

————. *Pennsylvania German Reverse Painting on Glass,* Home Craft Course, Vol 12. Plymouth Meeting, Pa.: Mrs. C. N. Keyser, 1943.

KEYSER, MILDRED. *Pennsylvania German Design,* Home Craft Course, Vol. 3. Plymouth Meeting, Pa.: Mrs. C. N. Keyser, 1943. Sketches and explanations of the origins of many traditional motifs.

LICHTEN, FRANCES. *Decorating the Pennsylvania German Chest,* Home Craft Course, Vol. 11. Plymouth Meeting, Pa.: Mrs. C. N. Keyser, 1948. Discussions of background colors and design for chests.

National Gallery of Art. *Index of American Design, Pennsylvania German Designs.* New York: Metropolitan Museum of Art, 1943. A portfolio of silk screen prints showing these designs.